Terry Hickland

Charland Publishing

Published by Charland Publishing 2020

Cover design by: Martin Kenny Design and Illustration

www.terryhickland.co.uk

ISBN: 978-0-9955058-1-0

To my dear mother-in-law Marina.

CHAPTER ONE

1987

"Ruairí, would you be a wee dear and fetch me a box of Sherbet Fountains?" requested his grandmother, Maeve Delaney, as she rang items through on the till.

"Where are Patrick and Kathleen?" asked her elderly customer, Peggy McGrath.

"Patrick's off to market in Birr with two of the pigs, and Kathleen has a doctor's appointment at the clinic."

"I hope it's nothing serious, Maeve?"

"No, just a slight chest infection."

"There's always something, isn't there? They don't make them like us anymore but maybe that's a good thing!"

Mrs McGrath cackled loudly as she opened her purse.

"That'll be twelve punts seventy, please, Peggy. Here, I'll help you pack your bag. Where's that useless husband of yours gone to?"

"Kevin will be picking me up when he's completed his urgent transaction at the bookies; he should be back soon. Ruairí, here's a little something for you, lad," said Peggy, as she handed him a punt before putting the rest of the change into her purse.

"Peggy, you'll spoil him!"

“Ach, they’re only young once! Sure how could you be bad to a wee face like that?”

“What do you say, Ruairí?”

“Thank you, Mrs McGrath,” murmured Ruairí as the blood rose to his cheeks, leaving them crimson.

“Ah, there’s the car now, I’d best be on my way,” said the woman.

“Mind how you go, Peggy. Say hello to Kevin for me.”

Maeve waved from behind the counter as her grandson held the door open.

“Ruairí, go and get those Sherbet Fountains before that money burns a hole in your pocket!” she said, as her grandson - remembering the chore he had been given - scampered off to fetch the sweets.

****

Ruairí lived with his parents, Patrick and Kathleen Delaney, above their store in the village of Ballinderry, Co. Tipperary. Maeve, who was Patrick’s mother, had built up a regular clientele over the years together with her husband John but, following his sudden demise, she had been left to look after the shop alone until it all became too much for her. At that time, Patrick was a guard in Portlaoise Prison and Kathleen worked at a supermarket in town. Being a prison warder had begun to lose its appeal, so the couple decided that they would relocate to Ballinderry.

Now ten years old, Ruairí was their only child. He was of thin frame, with raven-black hair, dark brown eyes and a swarthy complexion. A placid, affable youngster, he had never been any trouble to his parents. That day, he was helping out in the shop. He had been in the middle of cutting the wilting, yellow leaves off the cabbages on display in their wooden crates. The offcuts and rotten vegetables would help to feed the pigs that his father kept out the back.

"There you go, Nana. I brought a box of Mars Bars as well since we were running low on them," said Ruairí, setting the two cartons on top of the counter.

His grandmother looked down on him before placing a tender kiss on his brow. Ruairí didn't pull back. He liked these times alone with her, the gentleness, and the smell of the sweet perfume she wore.

"Come on, you, you'll need to be finished before your father gets home. He'll be wanting help with the far side of the barn. The sow is due her litter any day now and there will be babies to care for," she said, releasing her hold of Ruairí's head.

"Aw, Nana! Not more squealing piglets and their stinky straw to cart out!"

"They put food on the table and that's what matters," she replied, opening the boxes of sweets and positioning them on the shelves. "If you're good, your father might take you to market with him when he next goes."

"No thanks, I remember what happened the last time I went!" muttered Ruairí, as he reluctantly got back to trimming the cabbages.

A year ago, Patrick had taken his son to the animal sales yard in Birr. Ruairí had been wearing his best jeans, which got splashed by a cow doing its number twos as they walked around a pen. He wasn't keen on a repeat performance!

When Ruairí had no homework or chores to do, he would take his bike out on the local roads. An eight-year-old Raleigh Grifter, it wasn't much to look at but, when he was on it, he was Stephen Roche, his cycling hero. On those rare, longer trips when his father accompanied him, he savoured the feeling of the wind in his hair and the tails of his shirt trailing in the breeze.

In his mind, he'd be coming down the straight before Drominagh Woods, his legs going up and down like pistons as he tried to improve his lap time. Around the last bend, the spectators would all be cheering him on. He would have one final look behind as two of the other riders began closing in on him. Waiting for him would be his very own yellow jersey, sitting majestically on the podium, and all the important people would be present, including Father Moloney, the parish priest. They would hoist him up in the air for sure, before the pretty girls put the coveted trophy on him. He had made his mind up though that they wouldn't be kissing him as his mam was the only one allowed to do that, apart from his grandmother, of course!

Maeve lived in a quaint, chocolate-box cottage in the townland of Cornalack, near Ruairí's imaginary race circuit. It was a charming old dwelling, filled with the scent of lavender and homemade jam. At the age of sixty-eight, she valued her independence, owning a silver Toyota Corolla which was her pride and joy. She used the car to keep up on her social life, ferrying her friends to choir practice, getting to the shop and - during wintry spells when there was no bus - transporting Ruairí to and from school. Ruairí had never met Granda Delaney. Mam once said that the angels had visited his grandfather one day and that was the last anyone had seen of him. Ruairí was always wary now if Father Moloney came calling, in case he brought any angels with him. Whenever he did drop by, Ruairí would hide in the store at the back of the shop. It was full of mould and wolf spiders, their webs everywhere. No one in their right mind would want to look in there, he reasoned.

A short distance from Maeve's house was Lough Derg, part of the Galway-Tipperary waterway. Father Moloney, a tall man in his late sixties, with neatly trimmed grey hair, would tell those who attended Mass that the community was blessed to have so many people travelling from all over the world just to be in their tiny parish.

"Treat them with the dignity and respect they deserve. Respect them, respect them, that is all I ask of you," he would constantly urge.

Ruairí had always thought that Father Moloney's sermons were very dull. When he pointed this out to his mother one Sunday during Mass, she told him not to be insolent, explaining about all the important things the priest did for both God and the parish. Then, during Communion, she made him say twelve Hail Marys and four Our Fathers for being so disrespectful.

The family home had originally been constructed in the 1800s and had been extended before Ruairí was born, providing lots of nooks and crannies which were perfect for playing hide-and-seek. There was a false wall behind the wardrobe in his parents' bedroom; leaning back to rest there one day, he felt the panel move. His grandmother said it was a hide, made during the times when the Black and Tans came calling, and she went on to explain that they had been British mercenaries who were sent over to suppress the Irish people. When the 1916 uprising was taking place, the shop had been an undertaker's, and someone had once told him that the spirits of the dead, who had not been given a proper send off, had come back to haunt the house. As it cooled down during the night, Ruairí speculated that the creaking noises were really spirits darting about below the floorboards. He would quickly pop his head under the blankets at the slightest sound emanating from the eerie blackness of his room.

With the vegetables pruned, Ruairí went up to his room and took from the bedside table a copy of *Road Wheels* cycling magazine that his father had given to him. Plumping up the pillows on his bed for support, he lay back and began to peruse the various articles, as his Stephen Roche and Sean "King" Kelly posters smiled down on him benignly from the wall above.

Having studied the front cover, he went straight to the buy and sell section, looking at all the new and nearly new bikes for sale. There were so many lightweight aluminium frames and parts to choose from. It confused Ruairí no end. The prices were something he couldn't quite fathom either. He got an allowance of three punts a week and a bit extra during the holidays, when he had to work more. It would take forever to save up for something a little sportier than his Grifter.

CHAPTER TWO

Patrick walked into the livestock sales office, where industrial air fresheners hung from the wall to help diffuse the smell of effluent that had been traipsed along the floor by some of the farmers. He bumped into Brendan O'Riordan, who was waiting in line to register his cattle for the auction. Brendan and he had been best friends since childhood, only drifting apart when Patrick left for Portlaoise.

"Well, how are you, Patrick?" asked Brendan as they shook hands.

"As fit as a fiddle, thanks, Brendan," Patrick replied. "What have you for selling this fine day?"

"Four bullocks, though I don't imagine the price will be high, given the number of cattle here today. Have you brought a few porkers with you?"

"Just the two. The sow's ready to give birth any day now and I want this pair out of the way."

"So, you're here to make a sizeable return on your investment?"

"Ach, now that'd be tellin', Brendan, though I hear there's great demand for pork on the mainland."

"Talk's cheap, it's the gavel that will tell the tale, my friend. How's everyone back home then, making a wee fortune with the shop?" O'Riordan jested.

"We're keeping our heads above water, as long as no one opens one of those petrol station supermarkets and begins to undercut us. Give me a fair price and you can have the lot!" joked Patrick as the queue slowly inched forward.

Patrick had no regrets for leaving the prison service. At least both he and Kathleen would have a bit of a pension to share in later years. In the meantime, the store was providing them with a steady income.

"Listen, Patrick, if it wasn't for my Niamh and the Civil Service we'd be out on the street by now," said his friend. "Raising a family and trying to feed and clothe them isn't easy. I hope my four bullocks attract the bidders or she'll have my hide!"

"I know, Brendan," said Patrick, touching his friend's arm. "Look, will you go for a jar next Saturday night? You, Niamh, me and Kathleen. We'll get dressed up, have a meal and a few drinks at the Glass Boat Inn. Catch up on the gossip. What do you say?"

"That sounds like a grand idea! And sure the girls would jump at the chance to get their glad rags on. I'll ring you later and let you know," said Brendan, before the secretary called him over to take his entry details.

****

"Is this where you've been hiding, Ruairí Delaney? I thought you would have made a start on the barn," said Kathleen, having nudged his door open with her elbow whilst wrestling with a basket of ironing.

"I was just having a rest."

"Aye, I can see that. Rochey and Kelly didn't get to where they are today, just *having a rest*," his mother teased, putting away the clothes in his chest of drawers.

Spying the magazine, she sat down next to her son on the bed.

"Let's see now…. I wouldn't give that for a bike, I could buy a car at those prices!"

"But that's what all the top teams use to win with, Mam!" Ruairí argued, feeling a little deflated.

"I know, but where do they get the money for it? Five thousand punts for the frame! I would want it gold-plated at that price!"

Kathleen had watched Ruairí in recent months, riding his bike around the street. He had all but outgrown it, his knees nearly striking off the handlebars.

"What does everyone else have nowadays?"

"Mountain bikes," he replied, as he tried to study technical specifications.

"Which is better, a mountain bike or a street bike?" asked his mother cagily, trying to find out Ruairí's preference. Her friend's brother owned a cycle shop in Birr. With a little cajoling, she could get Ruairí a decent racing bike and pay it off in instalments.

"I wouldn't know, Mam, I've never been on a real racer," he said indifferently, waiting for the inquisition to end so he could read on in peace.

Her son could be difficult to get through to sometimes, Kathleen thought, as she tried once more to prise an answer from him. He was just like his father in so many ways.

"No, but listen to me, if you were on your holidays and had the choice, would you go mountain biking or road cycling?"

Ruairí looked up at his mother, unsure as to where her line of questioning was going.

"Mountain biking's for those who can't stick the pace of a road racer so I'd follow in the footsteps of Rochey and Kelly," replied her son with an air of confidence.

"Where did you find that mouthful, Ruairí Delaney? I'll have to speak with your teacher and see what books he's been giving you to read!" laughed Kathleen, ruffling his hair on her way out.

A racing bike it'll be then, she whispered to herself. It would be Ruairí's birthday in a couple of months and there would have to be a lot of research to find just the right bike for him. Almost eleven years old, where did the time go? she mused, as she stopped briefly at the hall mirror, tucking away a few grey strands of hair before returning to the shop, where her mother-in-law was readying herself to go home.

****

A few weeks later, Ruairí was in Terryglass National School with his friends, Oisín Halloran and Liam Kavanagh, a mutual love of

Gaelic football having brought them all together from an early age. As they sat on the steps outside the assembly hall, drinking fizzy cola and sharing out Midget Gems, Donal Fleming, a gangly youth with curly ginger hair, strode up to join them.

"Anybody got a snout?" he asked.

"You're so stingy, Donal. You never have ciggies, always on the scrounge!" replied Oisín.

"Ah, that's not true! Sure didn't I give some of you lot cigarettes last week?"

"Yeah, but only because you stole them from your mam!"

"If I tell you something, Oisín, will you give me a smoke during lunch break?"

"Depends. What's the gossip?" enquired Oisín, who had a keen dislike for Donal.

"Am I getting a smoke then?"

"Okay! Just get on with it!" shouted Oisín impatiently.

"Aidan's ma has run away with the guy who came to paint their house!" he exclaimed.

"Donal, you talk the biggest load of crap," said Oisín.

"It's true! The painting's only half done, and his oul fella has had to take time off work to look after the kids!"

At that moment, Aidan Donnelly walked through the school gates, his satchel over his shoulder, waving as he made his way over to the group. He was at least a foot bigger than Donal and was in the local boxing team. He could take anybody down, if he so chose to, in the ring.

"Who's going to ask him?" queried Liam.

"Donal's doing all the talking, let him do the needful," said Oisín, taking great pleasure in Donal's discomfort.

"Just drop it, Liam, he'll be in a bad way as it is. Maybe it's best to say nothing," Donal replied.

"Oh no, Donal, you started this!"

Ruairí watched as the charade was played out. Donal was looking around him, undecided whether to stay or run, his face red as a berry.

"Guys, don't.... let it drop.... please," he protested.

"How would you like someone calling your ma a slapper?" asked Liam.

As Aidan sauntered over to the group they all looked around, no one willing to touch upon the subject of his mother.

"Aidan...."

"Don't, Oisín!" begged Donal.

"Aidan, Donal here tells us your mother has been overly friendly with the painter at your house and that she ran away with him."

Donal was already through the doors of the assembly hall and bolting in the direction of the headmaster's office.

"Grab my bag, guys, I've had enough of him. The Care-Bear's going to be taught a lesson he won't forget in a hurry."

With that, Aidan went off in pursuit of his quarry.

"Did you really need to do that, Oisín?" questioned Ruairí as the group broke up.

"What's it got do with you, Delaney? Do you want to make something of it?"

"You just took it a bit far, is all I'm saying…."

Ruairí fell on his back as Oisín's fist struck his lip hard. Touching it gingerly, he saw blood on his finger. In a split second, they were both entangled, trading blows before being dragged apart by Headmaster Finlay, who marched them straight to his office.

****

"Explain yourself, Halloran!" demanded the head.

"He swung for me; it was self-defence…."

"He's a liar! I…."

"You'll have your chance to speak, Delaney. Well, Halloran, there were witnesses to the assault so tell the truth."

"He said things about my ma. I lost it, and hit him."

"That's not what I heard. You didn't agree with your colleague's viewpoint and you struck him, is that not so?"

Oisín just looked at his feet and remained silent, knowing the more lies he told the longer the suspension would be.

"Delaney?" probed the headmaster as he waited for Oisín's explanation.

Ruairí didn't want to get his friends into any more trouble than they already were as, unsurprisingly, Aidan would have given Donal a pounding after cornering him. Seeing that neither of the two was prepared to make a statement, Master Finlay had decided to summon the other boys' parents for an urgent meeting.

"I said nothing, sir, he just punched me for no reason!"

"Very well then, you may leave but I'll be watching you from now on, Delaney. You can let your mother know I shall be phoning her regarding this matter."

Oisín, Aidan and Donal were all suspended for the rest of the week. Ruairí was grounded and his father set him the task of cleaning out the storage room, cobwebs included.

CHAPTER THREE

The Delaneys and O'Riordans met at eight, in the restaurant of the Glass Boat Inn. The pub had been modernised over the years and consisted of a long bar with numerous snugs. At weekends, the restaurant doubled up for dinner dances.

"Welcome, everyone, the specials tonight are vegetable soup, grilled trout and braised lamb," said the waitress, who was dressed in the customary uniform of a black skirt and white blouse. "Would you like to see the wine list?"

"I'm going to treat myself to a glass of Liebfraumilch," replied Kathleen. "Niamh?"

"Ah, go on then, sure these two boyos are catching the tab, are they not? I'll have a glass too, please."

"Gentlemen, what will yourselves be having?"

"Oh, we'll just have to slum it, Patrick, and the girls can let their hair down. Two pints of Guinness, love," said Brendan, enjoying the banter.

****

"Well, Patrick, you heard right when you said the demand for pork in the UK and Europe had gone up!" exclaimed Brendan, as their empty dessert dishes were whisked away and they retired to the bar.

"Six hundred punts for the pair, which was much more than I'd reckoned on!" he whispered to his friend as they seated themselves in a vacant snug while their wives made straight for the powder room.

"It's hard to win, Patrick. If only you had kept the four you sold last month. They barely made half of what you got the other day," said Brendan.

"Ah, now, if only I had a crystal ball, wouldn't things be just rosy, Brendan. I'd pay off all my loans and I'd be away, sunning myself, and making plans to start rearing some of them rare breeds, like the Gloucestershire."

"If I had the money, I would leave agriculture altogether. Unless you're at it in a big way, it's a waste of effort, Patrick."

"Sure it's only a pipe dream, Brendan. Anyways, how's about another round? It'll be an hour or more before your brother picks us up. Girls, are youse up for another?" he asked as the women returned.

"Patrick Delaney, you're a very bad influence!" giggled Niamh, already rather tipsy, as Patrick went to the bar and ordered a last round.

****

Back at the house, Kathleen put the record player on, the spirit of the night still upon her. She placed a record by Big Tom and the Mainliners onto the turntable.

"It's been a lovely evening, darling," she whispered into her husband's ear as he held her in a warm embrace. "Niamh and Brendan were in excellent form. Where does he find the jokes?"

"Sure he's always been a right comedian, love. Now, be quiet and give us a kiss," he said, pulling her closer, his lips meeting hers.

They continued dancing late into the night, ending with another one of Big Tom's songs, *Gentle Mother*, before heading to bed.

****

There was a knock on the door the following Saturday night; Patrick had been expecting company.

"That'll be Seamus now," said Kathleen. "I wish you wouldn't take Ruairí out lamping, you know how I feel about it!"

Seamus Donnelly was a lifelong friend of the family and came from the townland of Ardcrony. Both he and Patrick had been lamping from no age with their own fathers, and they looked on the tradition as a rite of passage for their sons.

"But he's looking forward to going, love! It gives rain for the coming week and what we catch tonight will top up the freezer," replied Patrick.

"Don't be keeping him out too late. I worry when you're out there in the fields; anything could happen."

"Aidan's coming along too, and sure the exercise will do the lads no harm."

"Just mind yourselves," said Kathleen as she slid two apple pies into the oven.

Running down the stairs, Patrick answered the door.

"Seamus, I'll be with you in a jiffy, I just need to fetch Ruairí," he said, turning to run back up again.

The bedroom floor was littered with felt tip markers as Ruairí completed a sketch he had made of cyclists taking part in a race.

"How's it going, son?"

"Good.... What do you think of my drawing, Dad? I'm in second place and Kelly's leading."

"That's a fine piece of work alright! Listen, Seamus and Aidan are here, and they're raring to go. They tell me O'Meara's Acres are teeming with rabbits, eating all the crops."

"Yeah?" said Ruairí as he bolted out past his father, the felt tips scattering everywhere.

Patrick reached out and stopped Ruairí in his tracks.

"And remember to put on your wellingtons; you ruined your best trainers when you were last out!"

With gumboots and waxed jacket on, Ruairí shouted, "Bye, Mam!" as he attempted to get out the door.

"Ah, you're lucky, Mr Ruairí!" said his mother as she came out to check that he was suitably attired.

"Mam, stop fussing, we'll be late!"

"You be careful now," she warned, fastening the last button before she kissed them both.

"I will," he replied as he ran to his friend waiting in the jeep.

Kathleen watched as they merged onto the main road, the vehicle's headlights fading into the distance.

****

The foursome arrived at O'Meara's Acres as darkness fell. Parking down a lane, they walked close to the forest. Here they scouted around, searching for marks in the ground, evidence of well-used rabbit runs where they could set their snares. As the night wore on, they headed back to the open fields. The men unsheathed their hunting rifles, while Ruairí and Aidan carried powerful flashlights. With everything ready, they settled into the hedgerow and waited for the rabbits to come out to feed.

"How's Roisín doing? It must have been like a bolt out of the blue," said Patrick as the boys went to set more traps in the next field.

"The doctors gave her blood-thinning drugs which helped to break up the clot in her brain; it was a bit of an ordeal for sure. The kids are with my sister-in-law until Roisín's discharged from hospital, and I've had to take Aidan to work with me. The last thing I need is the guards at my door, looking to charge him with assault. I presume you've heard about young Fleming?"

"Ruairí said your lad knocked seven bells out of him."

"I can assure you he won't be doing that again! As if I didn't have enough on my plate, without that gormless sod telling everyone my missus was doing a line with the decorator. Christ, if the man hadn't been there on the spot and called the ambulance, we'd have lost her altogether."

****

"What did your da do about your scrap with Donal?" asked Ruairí, idly shining the light over the fields.

"I thought he was going to blow his top!" replied Aidan. "I've never seen him so mad. He threatened to beat the tar out of me if I ever hit anyone outside the ring again, and he meant it!"

"You're jammy! I thought you were for it, to be sure!"

"I don't care. Donal just can't go around making up stories. Will you shine the lamp so I can see what I'm doing, you plonker!"

"Hurry up, you big girl's blouse, even the rabbits are laughing at you!"

"If you don't shut up and hold that light still, you'll be eating rabbit blackberries!"

Having secured the snare, Aidan picked his way over the rabbit poo and half-chased his friend back to where their fathers patiently waited for their prey.

****

"Ach, sure he's the spit of his da. That lanky big drip couldn't hold his whist no matter how many hidings he got. Do you not mind the time we threw him stark-naked into the lake at Bushypark before we hid his clothes and made a quick getaway?" asked Patrick as the youngsters' dark silhouettes came ever nearer.

The two men burst into loud guffaws of laughter, the vision forever etched in their minds of the pale figure surfacing in his birthday suit with his curly mop of hair dripping wet, and dragging himself onto dry land.

“The big eejit was like a drowned rat, with his hands round his crown jewels, running about looking for his kit!” said Patrick, taking up the story.

“It was Brendan’s idea to hide his clothes in the bushes and scarper, after Fleming had elbowed him into the Derg the week before in his Sunday best,” Seamus added.

“It appears that the son has inherited his father’s daft ways,” Patrick observed, getting to his feet and pulling his friend up with him.

After a few hours, they had bagged thirty rabbits in total. With the snares packed in the rucksack and the rifles put away, they made their way back over the fields to the Land Rover. On their return home, Patrick hung his share of the night’s catch in a lean-to at the back of the shop, where Ruairí would prepare them for the freezer after Mass the following morning.

CHAPTER FOUR

"Will you lift the thing, Aidan!" ordered Ruairí, struggling under the weight of a large branch.

"It's Oisín's fault!" Aidan cried.

"I'm lifting it as high as I can!" exclaimed Oisín before they all let it fall to the ground.

The boys were in the middle of building a treehouse in the remains of a tall oak in the forest at Gurthalougha and were using branches as rafters, over which an old truck tarpaulin was to be draped, making the hide for the most part waterproof.

Two weeks ago, they had had a sleepover at Ruairí's, though there had been little sleep that night. With spring well underway, they had all decided that they would need a den in which to hang out over the summer holidays. Lying on top of thick blankets and bundled up in their sleeping bags on Ruairí's bedroom floor, they talked into the wee small hours, envisaging a wooden fortress, high up in leafy foliage. There had been more than just a few arguments over where the prime location was to be found, until Oisín reminded them of the oak tree that had been struck by lightning.

As a result of their late-night discourse, Aidan's father, who was the landowner's cousin, had obtained special permission for the gang to build the hide and play in the forest, provided there were no detrimental effects on the local flora and fauna.

To their great surprise, they caught sight of Donal heading in their direction across the fields.

"What does he want?" asked Oisín, as he finished tying the rope onto a log to be hoisted up into the tree. "He has a right cheek showing his face here."

After a few minutes, the straggly youth arrived, looking a little awkward and clutching a pink and green striped shopping bag.

"You're not welcome here, Fleming, shove off!" demanded Oisín, as Aidan stood with his hands forming fists.

"I just want to hang out with you all. I'm sorry, Aidan, for what I said about your ma, somebody told me that. I didn't mean any harm."

Oisín made a lunge for Donal, grabbing him by his shirt before Aidan got hold of Oisín and pinned him against a tree.

"You listen to me, Halloran, Donal has been big enough to apologise for what he said and that's alright by me. I should've given you a pasting for starting all this in the first place. Now you owe him an apology; tell him you're sorry!"

Raising his face slightly in a stand-off with Aidan, Oisín spoke.

"Let me go, Aidan, it's none of your business."

"It is when you're picking on someone for no reason," said Ruairí.

What's got into you? Say you're sorry or I'll give you a thumping!" demanded Aidan.

The friends all looked on helplessly as the pair stared one another out. Seeing that he was getting nowhere, Aidan loosened his grip on Oisín, who sauntered past him and the rest of the group. He purposely nudged Donal with his shoulder as he walked by, heading towards the fields. Before long, Oisín became a distant figure as he made his way home. Ruairí knew that Oisín would come back to them in his own time, but his friend's aggression of late troubled him.

"What's in the bag, Donal?" queried Aidan, seating himself on a fallen tree trunk.

"Yeah, what's in the bag, Flem?" asked Ruairí, trying to make their friend more at ease.

"Me ma gave me some spuds."

The group burst out laughing as Donal tipped out half a dozen raw potatoes. They had been banking on crisps, or a few packets of sweets at the very least. Leaving the bag in the treehouse, they all went for a stroll through the forest to the adjacent scrubland, in search of a rabbit to go with the potatoes. Ruairí and Liam walked on as the other two followed behind; their friends needed to sort out their differences.

After an hour or two of skirting the forest, they returned with some deadwood and made a fire. A little later, as the blaze subsided, the embers cast a red glow on their faces whilst they laid potatoes in the smouldering ash. A rabbit they had caught was already roasting on a makeshift spit. The potatoes ended up being a little burnt but, having forgotten all about their quarrels, no one was complaining as they tucked in.

The wind gently ruffled the canopy above, blowing ash over Mrs Fleming's shopping bag as it lay on the ground. Donal looked at the old, white-faced army watch that he had got from his father; that was the only thing regular about him, his punctuality.

"It's half five everyone, I need to be going. It won't be long before Da's home from work."

"Your da never worked a day in his life!" teased Ruairí as they found sticks and began to put the fire out.

"He works harder than yours, Delaney. That shop youse have is a cosy little number," he argued, as he kept up the banter, unsure whether to include Aidan in the ribbing.

"Come here, you big ginger eejit," said Aidan, as he put his arm around Donal's neck and proceeded to give him a Chinese rope burn on his wrist.

The pair grappled with one another until Aidan released his hold on Donal.

"Last one back to Ballinderry wears girls' pants!" Donal laughed, as they all raced across the fields, jumping over the wild tufts of grass.

****

A few days later, Ruairí, Oisín and Liam were having their afternoon lesson with Master Rankin. He was very strict and took absolutely no nonsense. Parents would frequently complain about the man's teaching methods but, given the high grades the students achieved, his conduct was generally overlooked. Ruairí had been out lamping with Aidan the previous night and was very weary. The airless room wasn't helping, and staying awake was becoming virtually impossible.

Rankin was writing figures on the whiteboard as pupils called them out to him from their study books.

"Eoin McGinty, what is six multiplied by twelve, divided by three?" he asked.

Eoin looked up from his book and was a little hesitant before getting up to answer.

"Twenty-four, sir?"

"Are you asking me or telling me? Twenty-four is correct. Now, another one, let's see," said the teacher, scanning the room. "Conor Ahern, you'll do. Eleven multiplied by twelve, divided by six."

Conor was very strong on English but had a little difficulty with mathematics. Rankin saw potential in his student and liked to test him, putting the lad on the spot.

"Come, come now, the day is growing shorter while my hair grows longer! What's the answer, Ahern?"

"Twenty-one, sir," he said tentatively.

"Wrong. It's twenty-two, you should have gotten that. Ruairí Delaney, eight multiplied by nine, divided by four."

Ruairí was fast asleep beside Liam, the late night and the heat of the room having caused him to doze off. Rankin scrutinised him closely before launching a duster in his direction. It bounced off a steel storage locker, startling him from his deep slumber.

"To the front!" barked the teacher. "Is the subject not stimulating enough for you, Delaney?"

Bleary-eyed, Ruairí just looked at the floor. No matter what he said, the teacher would want his pound of flesh.

"Well, what's your excuse for falling asleep then?"

"It's the room, sir, it's too stuffy in here," murmured Ruairí.

"And yet no one else appears to have conked out, Delaney. Take this marker over to the board!" ordered Rankin, as he lifted a textbook from his desk. "Divide forty-eight by twelve, multiply it by eleven and then subtract sixteen."

Ruairí feverishly worked on the calculation, rubbing out part of the sum and then correcting it.

"Twenty-eight, sir!"

Rankin, his dander already up, was a little disappointed that the youth had got the calculation right.

"A spot of detention will ensure you sleep when you're supposed to, and not during school hours."

"But, sir, I've Gaelic training and Master Flynn will be fuming if I don't show up!"

"I'm sure he'll manage without you, so let him know after class and be back here at three-thirty precisely. Now, go and sit down."

"Yes, sir," replied Ruairí, muttering under his breath as he returned to his seat.

He could put up with detention, but he didn't want his parents to know that he had been kept behind. If they did find out, that would put an end to his lamping for rabbits. What hurt the most - and Master Rankin knew this - was missing training. Apart from the cycling, Ruairí wanted, someday, to be picked for the county minors' league of the GAA. His grandmother had told him of all the matches that Granda Delaney had played in, and his medals and cups were in pride of place on the sideboard in her parlour.

****

Ruairí spent a rather dreary hour, working out mathematical problems from a past exam paper that Master Rankin had given him. While the teacher was engrossed in his *Irish Times*, he watched as his friends were put through their paces on the pitch. In his frustration, Ruairí swore silently, until he looked up at the crucifix on the wall and quickly said a prayer of contrition for his hostile thoughts towards the man.

When detention was over, he ran out of the building just in time to meet up with his mates as their parents came to pick them up. Liam's mum pulled up in her jeep and the two boys piled into the back, throwing their kit bags in the rear.

"Did you score any goals?" asked Ruairí in a low voice, in case Mrs Kavanagh overheard him and wondered why he would ask such a thing if he was at practice.

"No. Halloran scored two but was sent off for a foul, after O'Brien took a dive, the big nancy!"

"Sure I saw him, when oul Rankin wasn't looking. He'll get himself a bad name if he keeps cheating, and the county board scouts will soon pick up on it."

"We gave him a doing with our towels in the changing rooms, just for the craic," Liam sniggered as they pulled up at the Delaney house.

"See you tomorrow," said Ruairí, and he closed the door of the jeep and went inside, hiding his PE gear under the stairs, in case his mother found the unmuddied football kit and started asking awkward questions.

"Hi."

"Hello, my wee man," said Kathleen, drying her hands and coming over to hug her son. "Have you much homework?"

"Yes."

"Go and get changed, love, and then I'll make you some tea and toast."

Casting his bag aside, he went into his room. From the shop below, he heard Mozart being played. On this occasion, it was *The Marriage of Figaro* and the Countess was reflecting upon her unhappy marriage. From an early age, Ruairí had heard many of his works; he was one of his father's favourite composers, after Puccini. Patrick liked to listen to classical music when he was counting the day's takings, or on a lazy Sunday afternoon. Now wearing an old tracksuit, Ruairí followed the aroma of fresh toast and raspberry jam to the kitchen.

CHAPTER FIVE

"Ruairí, tell your mum I need more hot water," said Patrick, anxiously watching over the sow as she began to deliver her litter.

Ruairí rushed off to find his mother.

"Mam, Dad says he needs more hot water!"

"Is it not near time you were in bed? You've school in the morning, or have you forgotten?"

"But Dad says there will be a lot of piglets! Can't I help him? I promise I'll be up early enough."

Kathleen knew not to give in to Ruairí, even when he batted those big brown eyes at her.

"No, you're for bed and that's an end to it. I don't want to hear from your teacher that you've been sleeping in class!"

Ruairí immediately obeyed and went straight upstairs. He couldn't take the chance of Master Rankin calling his parents and telling them that he had fallen asleep on two separate occasions. That would be an end to his nights out lamping!

****

"This is going to be a long night, love. Did you get Ruairí off to bed?" asked Patrick, as Kathleen set down the bucket of warm water and poured her husband a mug of tea from a Thermos flask.

"Yes, despite his protests. You know what he's like, any excuse to stay up. How's she doing?"

"Exhausted, but getting through it somehow. She's no stranger to this," he said, washing his hands before taking a sip of the scalding beverage.

They worked on through the early hours until all the babies had been delivered, fourteen in all. On her way to bed, Kathleen looked in on Ruairí who had fallen asleep long ago, unable to fend off his weariness.

****

One Sunday afternoon, with the weather turning milder, Patrick decided to take Ruairí on an outing. The little Grifter was not cut out for the speeds his father's bike was capable of so they cycled at a leisurely pace, enjoying both the exercise and the countryside. After an hour, they stopped for a rest near the jetty at Coolbawn, where Patrick took out apples, Mars Bars and two bottles of Lucozade from his rucksack.

"Dad, what do Rochey and Kelly eat when they're racing?" asked Ruairí, unwrapping a Mars.

"Things with plenty of energy in them."

"Like what?"

"Things like we're eating now, with glucose to replace the calories that are burnt off as they travel along the race route. Although, it goes without saying that those boyos have the finest people around them, mixing up all sorts of potions."

Smiling, Ruairí looked at the chocolate bar and drink. His refreshments were just like those of the two big fellas in the posters on his bedroom wall!

When they had finished, the pair began skimming stones over the water.

"How many times did it bounce, son?" enquired Patrick, looking around the shoreline for suitable replacements.

"Three!"

"Is that all, Ruairí Delaney? You can do better than that!"

Patrick ran and lifted him up, pretending that he was about to throw him into the lake. Ruairí squealed, both with shock and enjoyment, as he was swung around in his father's arms, close to the water's edge.

"Here, let me show you how it's done," Patrick said, extracting a smooth pebble from his trouser pocket. The stone skimmed the water seven times before disappearing below the surface.

Ruairí practised under his father's instruction for an hour, with some success. All too soon, it was time to go. Dinner would be waiting for them.

****

"Oh, so you've remembered where you live then!" teased Maeve, as she set the table, while Kathleen began serving dinner.

"Nana, you should have seen us skimming on the Derg! I…."

"Never you mind about the Derg, Ruairí Delaney, go and spruce yourself up. And as for you, Patrick, you're worse than the child!" said Maeve, filling the glasses with juice.

The pair quickly scrubbed their hands and returned to the dining room, where grace was said. Ruairí tucked into the potatoes, bacon and cabbage, occasionally stealing a glance at his grandmother, unable to gauge how angry she was with them for being late. She caught him looking at her, and a frown of mock disapproval soon turned into a sly grin. That was his cue to tell of the day's events, of how he shifted some 'logs' - they were just branches to anyone else - that had fallen on the path leading to the water's edge.

"You should have seen them, Nana, they were massive! I couldn't leave them there for someone to trip over."

"You're so considerate, Ruairí, Father Moloney would be very proud of you. You know he's been asking if you would become an altar boy."

Ruairí froze, his mouth open and full of cabbage and potatoes, before he slowly turned and looked to his mother for help. Nana had once whispered in his ear that God told the priest about everything that happened in the parish. Did he know that Ruairí had insulted him? Taking a large gulp of juice, he cleared his throat.

"Do I have to, Nana? There are plenty of boys who could do it much better than me and anyway, I've got loads of training to do if I'm to be a bike racer," said Ruairí, desperately trying to get out of the awkward situation.

It was true that Father Moloney was looking for altar servers, he had said so at Mass in school, not two days ago. At the end of the homily, he had called out for volunteers and Ruairí, sitting three rows from the front in the assembly hall, hid his face behind a taller girl, in case the parish priest should decide to pick candidates for the job right there and then.

"You'll think it over, won't you, Ruairí?" said Patrick as his son, reassured by his dad's intervention, nodded, and finished his supper.

"It would be marvellous if you were to do it, Ruairí. Did you know that your grandfather was an altar boy when he was a lad?" asked Maeve.

Ruairí grunted in between mouthfuls, cramming as much food in as possible so that he could make a speedy retreat to his room.

"You'll be getting indigestion if you don't slow down, Ruairí. Take your time and eat properly. I'll speak with him later, Maeve," said Kathleen, changing the subject. "Ruairí, away and put on your pyjamas. I'll have your tea and a Wagon Wheel by the fire when you're done," she said, striking a match and placing it near the gas ring on the cooker to boil the kettle.

Readying himself for bed, Ruairí weighed up the pros and cons of being an altar server. Aidan had told him that most of those currently serving had been pressurised into it by their parents, and he hoped that his mam and dad wouldn't do likewise. As he tied the cord on his dressing gown, Ruairí ran to the sitting room and snuggled up with his father while waiting for their favourite television programme to start. His mother, bringing in his tea and biscuit, smoothed his hair and gave him a comforting smile.

****

Around nine o'clock, Maeve put on her coat to go home.

"A big kiss for your oul' Nana," she said, as Ruairí got up and wrapped himself around her.

She buried her face into the top of his freshly-laundered nightwear.

"You smell so sweet! Will you promise me something, Ruairí?"

"What, Nana?"

"Never grow up, pet, stay just the way you are," she said, clasping him in her arms.

"Ah, Nana, don't be silly, everyone grows up. That's why Mam feeds me so much. She says I need big strong bones if I want to be like Rochey."

There was a slight moistness around the old woman's eyes as she released her hold on her grandson. Maeve was very fond of Ruairí, who was a carbon copy of her late husband at that age. She said her goodbyes and left, dabbing her eyes with a silk handkerchief taken from her handbag.

****

Maeve placed the car keys on the intricately carved walnut console table in her hall, and stopped to bless herself at a holy water font. Apart from her family, God was her companion and comforter when alone. Fifteen years had not diminished the feeling of isolation she experienced as she pottered around at night. Patrick had asked her on many occasions to move in with them, but it was her husband's presence here that prevented her from doing so.

****

"Good morning, Maeve," said Kathleen, who was meticulously arranging packets of processed cheese in one of the many fridges at the back of the store.

"Hello, Kathleen, what a grand day it's to be. You can tell it's nearly April, Easter's not far away; the ladies are starting to plan the floral display for the church."

Every morning, for as long as her daughter-in-law could remember, Maeve had arrived at nine o'clock precisely and inspected the shop. After they had taken up residence in Ballinderry, she had gone without delay to the solicitors and signed over everything to Patrick but, after years of managing the business, it was still hard for her to let go.

As mothers-in-law went, Maeve was one in a million, thought the young woman, as she watched her put her blue work coat on and select a copy of that week's *Tipperary Star* so that she could pore over it, ready for the old busybodies and their salacious gossip of the day. Having disposed of the empty cheese carton out the back, Kathleen brought two mugs of tea over to the counter.

"What are you planning for Ruairí's birthday?" asked Maeve, idly thumbing through the Births, Deaths and Marriages column.

"As it happens, I was wanting to speak to you about that," Kathleen replied.

Maeve looked up and raised an eyebrow.

"Oh, really?"

"Patrick and I were mulling over the idea of a trip to Cork at Easter; would you like to come with us?"

"But who'd look after the shop if we were all away?"

"Niamh O'Riordan said she would take care of it for us. They're having work done to their kitchen, so they've no spare cash for holidaying this year."

"Does Ruairí know?"

"He doesn't, so keep it under your hat. Patrick found out that there's a charity bike race in aid of the local hospice in the city centre on Easter Monday. Stephen Roche and Sean Kelly are both taking part before they leave to prepare for the Tour de France."

"That sounds like a fantastic idea! Aye, I'll be happy to come with you all as long as you let me pay for the B&B."

"No, Maeve, this is our treat, I won't hear of you paying for it!"

"I insist, Kathleen. A little break will do us all a power of good. Drink up, there's that old windbag O'Dwyer coming. I'll go in the back until she's gone," said Maeve as she scurried away to the storeroom with her tea and the newspaper under her arm.

CHAPTER SIX

Liam and Ruairí were sitting in the treehouse at Gurthalougha Forest, unpacking the bags they had brought with them.

"Wow, you've got the latest Dandy, Ruairí!" said Liam excitedly.

"Aye, it came in yesterday, Liam."

"You're so lucky, having a shop. I'd be in the raspberry ruffles everyday if we owned it!"

"And, as my nana always says, you'd have no teeth left! You don't have to do all the dirty jobs, like feeding the pigs, and going into the store with all them wolf spiders looking at you."

"Ah, just squash them with an old, rolled up paper."

"I couldn't do that. They're God's creatures and need somewhere to live."

"Well, as long as they didn't bother me, I suppose. What else has your mam packed?" asked Liam, peeling an apple with his penknife.

Ruairí rummaged in the bag and threw him a packet of Perri potato crisps and a carton of orange juice before opening one himself.

"Your mam's the bee's knees!" said Liam as he leaned against the wooden plank, tucking into their treat.

"How do you think the seniors will do this year against Waterford, Liam?"

"Paste them, just like last year. Pierce Conlon will put them to shame again when he gets on the pitch!"

"My dad says he won't be fit enough to return because his injury still hasn't healed."

"Nah, he'll be back."

From below, there came the sound of a twig snapping; someone was walking towards their hide. Liam quietly crawled across the floor. As he looked out from the doorway, he was immediately hit in the face with water.

"Aidan, you git!" he complained, rolling back and wiping his face with his shirt tail as Ruairí fell about laughing.

Having climbed the tree, Aidan continued spraying his friends with a water pistol he had just bought.

"Too hot for you, lads?"

"Stop it, Aidan, you'll ruin my shirt and me mam will have your guts for garters!"

"Sure it's only water!"

He gave his friends one more dousing before putting the pistol in his coat pocket and sitting down opposite them.

"Is there any more grub for me or have you greedy sods eaten it all?"

"You don't really deserve anything, Aidan," said Ruairí, throwing him a bag of crisps.

"Where's lanky Fleming? He was away sharp today."

"His mam took him to get his eyes tested. He's been having headaches and Master Rankin's been complaining about the marks he's been getting for his homework," explained Liam, in between slurps of juice from the carton Ruairí had passed to him.

"Ah, sure he's a bit slow at the best of times. God help whoever gives him a job in the future," declared Aidan.

"Tell us something we don't know.... Has anybody heard about Oisín lately? That's two weeks he's been off; is he on the mitch?" enquired Liam.

"Nobody's seen him, not even in the village," added Aidan.

Ruairí spoke up.

"Listen, if I tell you this, you must promise not to say where you heard it from!"

The others turned to him in amazement. Ruairí Delaney was not known for making speeches or delivering gossip, so any announcement from him got their undivided attention.

"Okay," they replied in unison.

"No, I mean it, you both tell no one or I'll keep it to myself!"

"Tell us, Ruairí. Liam, you open your mouth and it's the Derg for you, with your clothes on!" commanded Aidan.

Liam nodded sheepishly. He knew it was not an empty threat.

"I was shifting old boxes and junk from the store in the assembly hall when I heard Master Flynn talking with Headmaster Finlay. You know that Oisín would rarely do sports and always had a letter from his parents saying that he was sick?"

"He's just a lazy ass, there was never anything wrong with him," said Liam.

"Apparently, Flynn had had enough of the excuses. He made him get changed for football practice and saw bruises while Oisín was putting his kit on!"

"He was probably talking instead of listening as usual, throwing his weight around once too often. He's too ready with his fists; someone must have given him a pasting," countered Aidan, in a dismissive tone.

"After the match, the PE teacher took him to one side to try and find out what was going on. Oisín wouldn't tell for a while but, with a bit of coaxing, he eventually got it out of him."

"You heard all this? Did Flynn forget you were there?" Liam asked.

Ruairí hesitated. He shouldn't have said anything to his friends. What if it got back to his parents? He would be in real trouble then. He shouldn't even have been listening in the first place. How he hoped God wouldn't tell Father Moloney; the confession box would be ringing with Hail Marys and Our Fathers by the time he was finished with him.

"Come on, Ruairí, don't stop at the juicy bit. Who gave him a panning?" quizzed Aidan.

"It was Oisín's dad, when he'd had too much to drink. The head said he was taken into care and that's why he's been absent."

"It'll be the Social that has him, probably put him with another family."

"So, he's not in hospital?" asked Ruairí, a little confused as he'd thought that being taken into care meant being looked after by the nurses at the hospital.

"No, he's with Social Services, and that's probably what has been the matter with him this last while. His oul fella's been knocking seven bells out of Oisín, the helpless sod!" explained Aidan.

Ruairí felt sorry for Oisín. He could not even begin to imagine being taken away from his family. Now that he thought about it, Oisín had really changed these last few months. Why were people so unkind? Ruairí's parents drank alcohol but it didn't make them want to punch him. Yes, he did get a clip on the ear occasionally, but his dad said that it was for being smart with him. Perhaps Oisín had been misbehaving and his dad had had enough. Ruairí couldn't make his mind up about his friend.

As clouds began to roll in from the west, they all reluctantly got to their feet.

"I'm heading on, Mam will be looking for me," said Liam, climbing down the tree first.

"Aye, we should all be going," said Aidan, viewing the ominous dark sky which signalled rain.

By and by, they were walking over the fields, in deep discussion about what they would be doing that night when they got home.

****

“Where are we going, Nana?” asked Ruairí as he helped the old woman pack his suitcase, while his parents carried out last minute jobs in the shop.

“I can’t tell you that, as I’ve been sworn to secrecy but, suffice to say, you’ll love it!” she said, folding his clothes so that everything would fit.

“I suppose so, but I need to know where it is, in case there’s something I have to bring with me,” insisted Ruairí, frustrated that no one had included him in the planning of this big adventure.

Ruairí thought long and hard as to where they all might be heading. Their last holiday had been in Killarney and, before that, it was a place called Blackpool, in England. He had been much younger then, still being transported around in a buggy. His friends asked him why he had never got to see the ‘black pool’ which, for a long time, Ruairí had believed was an enchanted pond at a sorcerer’s house just outside of town.

“Take one of your books and a favourite toy; if you behave, I might treat you when we get there. Now, hurry up, we need to be leaving soon,” she said, snapping shut the catches and carrying the case down the stairs and into the hallway.

Ruairí looked at her, confused.

“Hold on, it’s my birthday tomorrow. How will I have a party with my friends if I’m away?”

“Well, we’ll have to deal with that later. Come on downstairs and help your parents, my wee man.”

Pausing on every step, Ruairí's mood grew dark. He had a party every year. All of his pals came over and the craic was mighty. Now, out of the blue, they were going away and telling him nothing. Was he so unimportant that they weren't bothering to let him know where this great holiday place was? He elbowed open the door leading into the shop, causing it to hit the wall, which distracted him momentarily from his objective of asking his parents what was going on.

"Ruairí Delaney, what sort of an entrance is that? Are you trying to take the door off its hinges?"

He ignored his mother, his foul mood tempered a little by examining the door and the wall in case he had damaged them. Just then his father walked in.

"And what are you looking so grumpy about? We're all going on holiday, and you should be over the moon!"

"No one told me. I'm the last person to know anything around here!"

"Ach, now, Ruairí, don't," said Kathleen soothingly as she came around the counter.

"But my friends can't come to my party if we're going away!" he quavered, his emotions beginning to get the better of him.

"There's always next year," explained his mother, trying to calm him, before he ran back to his room.

Kathleen followed her son and found him kneeling on the old ottoman at the window, with his head in his hands. She went over and put her arms around him but Ruairí remained rigid, ignoring his mother's comforting touch.

"What's wrong with you? Sure it's just this once, and you'll have just as much fun where we're going. There'll be people you like and we'll have a big cake for your birthday."

"I don't want to talk about it," he whispered, his eyes trained on the field across the road.

Kathleen left him and returned to the shop, where she had arranged to hand over the keys to Niamh before they set off.

Tears began to roll down Ruairí's face. Aidan, Liam, Donal, and Oisín, none of them would be there for his birthday. What was so important that he couldn't have his party at home? He was utterly perplexed by his parents' decision. Taking a tissue from the box on the bedside table, he dried his eyes, trying to come up with a reason to postpone the trip for one more day.

CHAPTER SEVEN

"Ruairí, get down here now!" yelled Patrick, his agitation apparent as he waited at the foot of the stairs.

His son eventually appeared, dragging his feet as he descended the staircase. This was going to be the worst birthday ever.

"Go in and make sure there are no empty boxes in the store. If there are, take them out to the barn and don't be disturbing the piglets," he said as he went into the shop.

They care more for those piglets than they do for me, muttered Ruairí under his breath, walking through the shop, ignoring everyone. *And those spiders better not be about for their own sake; I don't need any more annoyance*!

He turned the Bakelite handle on the heavy cream-coloured door, then, giving it a hefty shove, it swung open. Ruairí managed to catch it before it hit the wall; he was in enough trouble with doors today. Walking behind a row of shelves, he came to an abrupt halt. There, in front of him, was a silver Raleigh ten speed racing bike, straight out of a brochure. Who could have left it there? Who owned it?

Patrick, having quietly followed Ruairí in, put his hands on his son's shoulders.

"Go on, Ruairí, it's all yours. Happy birthday from your mam and me."

Speechless, Ruairí hugged his father tightly as fresh tears stung his eyes, having received the one thing he had always asked for in his prayers. God must have turned a blind eye and not told Father Moloney about all of his sins after all!

"You can take it for a spin, Ruairí, while we finish up. Just down to the next lane and back though, do you hear?" ordered Patrick.

Nodding his head, Ruairí put on the helmet that had been placed on the saddle. Kicking up the stand that was supporting the bike, he took it outside and tried the brakes; they were sharper than the old Grifter. Throwing his leg over the crossbar, Ruairí placed his feet on the pedals and began to rotate them. Patrick, running behind him while holding the rear of the seat to get him started, let go, allowing him to roll down the road. Now seated, Ruairí began to familiarise himself with the gears.

Watching the pair from the upstairs window, Kathleen smiled as Patrick ran alongside his son, helping him figure out the workings of the bike. The shop owner in Birr had been so accommodating, helping her choose the right size of bike for Ruairí that would last him as he grew older.

Six hundred yards down the road and he was flicking it through the ratios. Roche was in his element now, leaning the Raleigh lower and lower, more so than he had ever dared to do on the old bike.

A sharp bend was fast approaching and Ruairí was in danger of overshooting it. Unfamiliar with their efficiency, he pulled the brakes on as hard as he could and the wheels began to lock up. Nearing a standstill, he put both feet down to steady the bike, just as he was about to fall into a hawthorn hedge. Ruairí got off and composed himself. Turning the bicycle around to head for home, he decided that he'd taken enough risks for one day.

With the sun now on his face, he was overjoyed that his parents had not forgotten his birthday. They had played such a big trick on him, even Nana. Yes, he would still miss his friends and not having a party like they had in the past, but where were they going for their holidays?

****

They set out just after two in the afternoon. It was pleasantly warm as they slowly made their way into Cork, the traffic being exceptionally heavy due to roadworks. Ruairí, having woken from a nap, rubbed his eyes to get a better look as to where he was being taken. His *Team Ireland* racing cap was lying at an off angle and, having corrected it, he wound down the window of the car, the cool breeze coming as a welcome relief. Looking up, he saw bunting suspended from every street lamp, along with copious amounts of flags and banners.

"Why are all the decorations up, Dad, what's going on?"

Kathleen turned around in her seat. It would be nearly impossible to keep the real reason for why the city was wearing her finest from him.

"So, you're finally awake then! You've been asleep for an hour now, so you'd better not be kicking about half the night, young man!" warned Kathleen.

“There’s seems to be a carnival on, son,” added Patrick.

A car in front of them stopped to let another vehicle access the road. Ruairí s eye caught a sign that had been pasted to a telephone exchange box.

“Dad, are Rochey and Kelly racing in Cork?” he enquired, as he just about got the words out, so great was his excitement.

His parents rolled their eyes at one another; it seemed that they had just been rumbled.

“I don’t know, are they?” replied his father.

“I just saw them on a poster! Is that where we’re going?”

“We’re already in Cork, son,” he explained.

“They’ll be here by now and, God willing, we’ll get a chance to see them,” his mother added.

“Nana, did you know about this?” asked Ruairí. “You did, you did!” he laughed, as he turned to read the billboard once more.

Patrick had received a copy of the race route from the promoters. All the riders would set off from pits located at the Opera House. They would then carry on down the straight in the direction of St Finbarr’s Hospital. Turning east, they would head towards Blackash and, past Nenaan Park, there would be sprints for position as they came to Wellington Bridge. Here the hard work would begin, right up to the finish at the Tyndall National Institute.

“Dad, you’re such a big fibber!”

Patrick maintained his poker face whilst checking the rear-view mirror. The traffic began to edge forward once again.

"I don't know what you mean, son!"

Ruairí hit his father on the head with an inflatable mallet that Maeve had bought him at a garage when they had stopped for fuel.

"You all knew about this, didn't you?" quizzed Ruairí, as one of the racing teams' cars emerged from a petrol station.

"It was an extra special birthday treat for you so we had to keep it under wraps," his mother answered. "I'm sorry, but we couldn't afford to bring all your friends."

His parents were the kindest, most loving people he could ask God for. They had bought him his new bike and now he was so close to his heroes. Aidan, Liam, Donal, and Oisín would just have to wait, there were more important matters to attend to.

"And I'm sorry for misbehaving earlier," said Ruairí sheepishly, as he pulled the cap over his eyes.

"You're a wee rascal," replied Maeve, ruffling his cap.

He gave her a mischievous grin while his mother looked back and smiled at him.

****

The Delaneys arrived at a bed and breakfast on Church Street, which was on the outskirts of the city but within walking distance of the main event. Patrick had a family ticket that gave them access to the riders at the end of the race. Ruairí helped his grandmother carry her luggage up the winding staircase and into her room, and then went back to assist his parents.

"Take your bag and your coat up to your room, pet," requested Kathleen as she collected more of their belongings from the boot.

"Which room is ours?"

"You and Nana Maeve are sharing."

"But Nana snores!"

"Ruairí, don't be so impudent! These were the only rooms left and there's just one bed in our room so we'll all have to grin and bear it."

Ruairí did as he was told, and made his way back indoors.

"And what's your name?" asked a woman, appearing from one of the rooms with a pile of tablecloths.

"Ruairí."

"Well, Ruairí, you have the most beautiful brown eyes I have ever seen! I hope you enjoy your stay in Cork."

"Thank you," he replied.

She reeked of garlic, he thought, as he climbed the staircase. And she had a moustache! Women weren't supposed to have moustaches, were they? Maeve had already unpacked and was brushing her hair.

"I thought you'd gone back to Ballinderry, you were away for so long. Come on, then, let's get your bag emptied and, after that, you can freshen up."

He rolled his eyes at the mere idea; it was only five o'clock and bath time wasn't until eight. Even so, he meekly handed her his clothes which she placed into a large dresser. Ruairí took his comics and toys and put them on the bedside cabinet. He knew this was the side he was to sleep on as the other unit was full of his grandmother's makeup. How embarrassed he got when women kissed him; they always left lipstick marks all over his face! Why they did it in the first place was a complete mystery, just like when someone called to the house unexpectedly and his mum would complain of it being in no fit state for guests.

Having unpacked all of their luggage, they then made their way on foot into the city to get something to eat. Workmen were still busy erecting barriers on the streets, to keep people off the track. Ruairí pulled himself up and, dangling over the rail, he looked down the avenue, visualising Rochey and Kelly thundering along neck and neck, toing and froing and trying to get by one another.

"Come on, son," urged his father. "Hurry up, before there's no food left."

Tomorrow was the big day, and Ruairí hoped they would have a superior vantage point from which to see the cyclists as they raced through the city, but he was secure in the knowledge that his dad somehow always came up trumps. They chanced upon a little café on St Patrick's Hill and went inside.

"Mam, I've got to have a wee!" said Ruairí, dancing around with his legs crossed.

"Why didn't you go before you came out?" she whispered. "Patrick, Ruairí needs to use the gents, would you take him?"

Ruairí went into a cubicle and, closing the door firmly behind him, stood there with his hands joined.

Dear God, Mam says it's wrong to ask for things but, just this once, will You help me out? Can I see the guys? I won't ask You for anything ever again, I promise. Thank You, God. Amen.

When he was done with his silent prayer, he blessed himself and flushed the toilet.

"Are you all sorted now, Ruairí?" asked Patrick as they returned to their table.

His son just grunted, pulling a menu in front of his face to hide his embarrassment at praying in a toilet cubicle. Father Moloney did say that God was everywhere and he had urgently needed to speak to him in private. After all, Nana always said that a problem shared was a problem halved. They ordered sausage and chips, with buttered bread, and a pot of tea. When their meal was over, they went for a walk by the River Lee, where they came across a little pub with live traditional music playing.

After a few hours, they headed back to the bed and breakfast. It was an early start the next morning if they wanted to get into the VIP area, as the tickets were on a first come, first served, basis. True to his mother's prediction, Ruairí had been unable to settle, his head full of the race the next day. Maeve Delaney, too, got precious little sleep, losing count of the times she was kicked in the back by her wriggling grandson.

CHAPTER EIGHT

It had rained the night before and the streets had a damp sheen to them as Ruairí looked out of the bedroom window. Nana was taking a shower, singing *Can't Take my Eyes off You* at the top of her lungs. He got out of his nightclothes and into a pair of jeans that had been laid out for him, waiting patiently on the bed in his white vest for her to finish. For as night became day, she would soon have him at the vanity unit, giving him a thorough going-over with a facecloth. His armpits were always top priority and, once satisfied that he was squeaky-clean, she would apply a liberal dose of spray deodorant.

"Are you looking forward to the race, wee man?" she said, drying him off with a rather coarse towel.

"That's sore!" he complained, before answering. "Yes, Nana, I am, though I guess we won't get to see Rochey and Kelly; there will probably be too many people there."

"Don't you be worrying your head about that now. When we arrive, you hold my hand tightly and we'll elbow our way to the front."

"But we can't do that, can we, Nana?"

"Sure who wouldn't let a little old lady and her grandson past them?" said Maeve, as she smiled lovingly at him; that face was of her husband when he was young.

"Did you two sleep in?" asked Patrick, buttering his toast.

"Come and sit here, Ruairí, I'll get you some corn flakes," said Kathleen, as she rose from her chair and went over to the food table.

"Dad, will we get to see them?" said Ruairí, as he polished off his orange juice.

"We'll have to get our skates on if we are to find a good place," his father replied, downing the last of his coffee. "I'll see you all in ten minutes; I need a shave."

Kathleen finished her breakfast and hurried Ruairí along. Whilst they had tickets for the VIP area, they still needed to get there before the roads closed for the race. The finish line at the Tyndall National Institute would be packed with people and press, so they ought to be on their way. It was already eight-thirty and the race started in an hour.

Walking down the street with his family, Ruairí could hear music playing loudly. Cars with sponsors' logos were passing to and fro. One of them had a poster of Stephen Roche on it. How he longed for one of those! *Would it be greedy to want an autograph on it as well?* he pondered. Ruairí pulled his zipper up to his neck to keep out the stiff breeze as they crossed the bridge, the River Lee surging below them.

As they came closer to the event, there was bunting everywhere and girls in bright coloured racing suits were handing out caps and keyrings. Ruairí tried to steer Maeve towards them but she was sticking rigidly to her chosen path.

"Dad, they're giving away souvenirs! Can we go back?" pressed Ruairí.

"We haven't time, son, we need to get to the finish stage soon or there will be no spaces left!"

Ruairí looked down Western Road.

"But there are spaces here! Won't they be coming this way?"

Patrick humoured Ruairí by looking down the road as well, in an attempt to pacify him. As parents, they were nearing their own finish line and he wasn't about to give the game away.

"Come on this way, son, I know a better place. If we're in luck, they might be handing out freebies there too!"

With such reasoning, Ruairí decided to accept his father's advice and continue on. The street vendors were out in force, with hamburger stands, trinket sellers, and even a beer tent. Ruairí noticed a flyer advertising a fortune teller. His grandmother had often spoken of these people being able to read your future with tea leaves but he could never see how, no matter how many times it was explained to him. Ruairí was fairly certain that the dregs at the bottom of a teacup could not predict what lay ahead for anyone!

They came upon an area that had been cordoned off from the main track. Ruairí read the notice as they waited in line; it stated that it was only for VIP ticket holders. Now they would have to make their way back to Western Road, he fumed, all because his father wouldn't listen to him. To top things, Patrick and Kathleen had started arguing but, whatever it was about, it could not be as important as getting a good viewing point for the race. Maeve wasn't much help either, as she held his arm in a vice-like grip. Ruairí pushed his hands deeper into his pockets.

He saw his mother bring out what seemed to be pink cards from her cavernous handbag. Why women needed such bags was yet another mystery to him. He had less things in his schoolbag. The official ripped the cards in half and opened the barrier to let them through. Ruairí was confused now; no one had mentioned tickets, never mind being allowed into the VIP area.

Up ahead were rows of promotional racing bikes, next to the manufacturers' tents. Maeve released her hold on Ruairí and he ran straight towards them, his mouth wide open, staring at these things of beauty. Patrick came over and, after having a quiet word with one of the representatives, lifted his son onto a bike.

"Ruairí, will you stop fidgeting!" Patrick ordered, as he prepared to take a snapshot of him sitting on a bicycle neither of them could ever afford. "Say *cheese*!"

"Chicken!" he replied, the flash of the camera leaving him temporarily blinded.

The next couple of hours were a melee of commentary coming from loudspeakers and the crowd surging towards the barriers each time the riders came by. In spite of his earlier worries, Ruairí had an unobstructed view of the competitors. At one point, he was left dejected when it was reported that Stephen Roche had been in collision with an Italian rider and had crashed. Later however, he came hurtling by, his legs rotating at a rate

Ruairí believed he could never match. Roche checked on the opposition, mentally noting how much of a lead he had on them, and briefly scanning the crowd.

Did he see me? Ruairí wondered, feeling that the big man must surely have noticed him, so close was he to the barrier.

As predicted, Stephen Roche was crowned the winner, followed by Sean Kelly and a French rider. Ruairí was now on his father's shoulders, such was the throng of people trying to see the prize-giving ceremony.

Following the awards, Roche stepped off the podium and came over to speak with the crowd, pausing in front of Ruairí to shake his hand.

"And what's your name?" he enquired.

Nervously, Ruairí told him.

"Do you like road racing, Ruairí? Are you thinking of taking it up?"

Ruairí could just about answer his hero, as his mother thrust forward a race cap in the team's colours for an autograph.

"Yes, Mr. Roche, I like it a lot and I hope to be a racer when I'm older," he stuttered, before Stephen engaged in conversation with other spectators.

Patrick positioned the hat on his son's head and took a family photo. As the event ended, the crowds began to filter through the barriers, heading into the city centre and the many bars.

"Mam, would you put my cap in your bag for safekeeping?" asked Ruairí as he handed his mother his now most prized possession, next to his new bike.

"Are you sure you trust me with it?" she replied.

"Don't squash it, please," he begged.

His idol had not only held the cap, he had signed his name on it; Ruairí was determined that this memento of his day would remain in pristine condition. He intended to make room in his bottom drawer, where it could be stowed out of sight. Aidan, Liam and the gang could look at it but there would be no touching, especially where Donal was concerned.

"Give it here," she said, taking out her scarf to make room for his trophy.

"Sure would you not like me to look after it?" his grandmother teased, hugging him.

"Thanks, Nana, but Mam's bag is safe enough. Dad, can I have a hamburger?"

"The food here is too greasy, we'll find somewhere better, Ruairí," said Kathleen, closing the buckle on her bag.

Her son slid his hand into hers. For Ruairí, this was the most amazing day of his life. Nothing really mattered now; it could rain for the rest of the week and he wouldn't care.

"Mum," he said, looking up at her.

"Yes?"

"You and Dad are really good at playing games."

“What do you mean, pet?” she asked innocently as they crossed the road.

“You know! You had all of this planned, the tickets and all for the *Very Important People* area. You two were awfully sneaky, but thanks ever so much.”

Kathleen looked adoringly at her son. For all their troubles, they had been blessed with their child. Bending low, she gave him a big hug. Ruairí was unable to see the solitary tear trickling down her cheek. He put his arms around her neck; she was wearing the perfume he liked best and little gold earrings.

“It wasn’t easy to pull it off,” she said as she got up. “Your father had to take out his book of magic and cast a few spells!”

“Mam, I’m eleven now! I know there are no such things as wizards and spells but it was class anyway. I didn’t realise Rochey was so big!”

“Don’t worry, you’ll be just as tall and just as handsome!”

“Mam!” said Ruairí, embarrassed, darting off to catch up with his father.

“He’s growing up fast,” commented Maeve, sidling up to her daughter-in-law on the crowded street.

“Don’t remind me!” snapped Kathleen, before she could stop herself.

“I’m so sorry, I didn’t mean it to come out as it did,” said Maeve apologetically.

“No, I’m the one who should be sorry, Maeve. You’re right, he is growing up fast.”

The pair locked arms as they followed father and son down the walkway.

"Ruairí's a wee gem, there's no mistaking, but in another couple of years it'll be his mates he'll be looking to go on holiday with," said Maeve.

"Will you give over your moaning, Maeve Delaney," laughed Kathleen, her mood lifting.

They hurried after Patrick and Ruairí, who were inspecting the menu posted on the window of a restaurant.

****

The remainder of the week was spent sightseeing and scouring practically every shop in Cork, looking for Maeve's favourite perfume without finding a single bottle. At Fota Wildlife Park, a short drive from the city, Ruairí was entertained by a multitude of animals that he had only ever seen in books or on television. The lemurs were his favourite because they would run and jump on the ropes for ages. At the chimpanzee enclosure, a chimp flung what Ruairí thought was mud that nearly hit his nana. He could see she wasn't impressed, as he heard her say a naughty word a little too loudly.

Lying in bed on the last night of their holiday, Ruairí reminisced about the week they'd had. Stephen Roche's handshake was so strong, he thought his hand would fall to pieces if he let go. When he got back, he would make himself some weights, so his arms would bulge like Rochey's. Ruairí couldn't wait until the prints came back from the chemist's. Nana had promised to buy him a special frame, a silver and black one, to display his favourite photograph in. He looked over at her, as she slumbered peacefully, dead to the world. He, too, would have a good night's sleep tonight.

CHAPTER NINE

The car was nearing Ballinderry; the holiday had ended much too soon. It suddenly dawned on Ruairí how much he had missed his friends, even Oisín Halloran. The gang had not seen Oisín for nearly a month, and the gossip was that he and his mam had gone to live with his aunt until they found a new house. The buds on the trees were beginning to open, he noticed, as he looked out of the window. He couldn't wait for summer to come; no school and the forest all to themselves.

With the car parked and the boot lid raised, they began to take their luggage in. Maeve couldn't resist stopping by the shop.

"Well, look at the cut of you, Maeve Delaney, and the quare colour you've got yourself in Cork!" exclaimed Peggy McGrath.

"Get away with you, Peggy!" laughed Maeve as she went behind the counter. "Well, Niamh, how are things? Were we busy?" she asked, sifting through the receipts in the till.

"Busy enough, Maeve…. My, you did get a bit of colour alright!" observed Niamh.

The old lady feigned indifference to the comment, even though she had only that morning looked in the mirror while getting ready to leave the B&B and had admired the golden tone of her skin.

Peggy beckoned her friend to the end of the counter, to tell her of some great secret the world was about to hear next.

"What's bothering you?"

"You've a new neighbour on the lake!"

"Would you talk sense, woman, whoever has come to our fine shores matters nothing to me. Sure don't we get countless tourists?"

"I don't know her name, only that she's Dutch and owns a barge moored at Coolbawn Quay."

"She has a right to live wherever she wants, as long as she pays the rates, isn't that so?"

"Aye, sure enough, but John Hewitt has taken it upon himself to organise a committee and has written to the council and the Birr Gazette!"

"That old fool has nothing better to do with his time than to interfere in other people's affairs. Dutch, you say?"

Ruairí had been sitting on the stairs, having carried the last of the baggage into the dining room where Kathleen was beginning to unpack, for this being Saturday was washday. He knew that he shouldn't be eavesdropping but who was this Dutch lady they were talking about? Ruairí's curiosity had already been fuelled.

Running to find his mother, he almost collided with her.

"Take it easy or you'll have us both in hospital before the day is over. What's the rush, have you not had enough action for one week?"

"Can I go out on my new bike? It won't do it much good just sitting there," he reasoned, twirling the door handle whilst staring intently into his mother's eyes.

"Put a coat on and make sure your helmet is fastened. Don't be speeding; you're not used to that bike and it's a lot faster than the old…."

"Mam, I'll never get out if you keep on giving me orders!"

Ruairí regretted the words as soon as he had said them. Through his impatience, they had come out all wrong.

"I'm sorry, Mam, I wasn't trying to be cheeky. Can I go now…. please?"

"A wee scallywag, that's what you are! Out of my sight with you but be back here in one hour as I'm making a fry for our tea."

"Yes, Mam!" shouted Ruairí, who was already on his way.

It was too late to get Aidan to help him investigate Coolbawn Quay. Mr Hewitt was very cantankerous, he knew that much. The whole gang had been out on their bikes once and had cycled up to the quay. They had begun to ask the Englishman about his boat and his life sailing the great oceans when, in a condescending manner, he had ordered them off the jetty and told them not to come back.

They didn't like him, that they were all agreed upon, thought Ruairí as his speed increased along the deserted country road. The bike was everything he had hoped for. The gears would take a little getting used to, but Ruairí enjoyed the thrill from the faster speeds achieved.

Lost in thought, he nearly came off the Raleigh as it entered a tight bend. If a car had been coming the other way, he would have been a goner, he felt, blessing himself. Nana's cottage looked so lonesome with no one there. The grass was beginning to grow and before long he would be called out to cut it. Approaching the end of the road, Ruairí dismounted and walked along the narrow footpath that bordered the lough. He lifted the bike over the turnstile - not wanting it out of his sight for a minute - and wandered along the jetty. He spied John Hewitt's boat. It wasn't anything special, just a tired old cabin cruiser. There were much more imposing vessels moored there.

Some distance away was the biggest boat Ruairí had ever seen. It was long and wide, and he was baffled as to how they had managed to get it to Coolbawn. He edged forward to take a closer look. The hull was black, the upper half white and the name, *The Johan*, was painted in orange.

There was a sudden clatter of plates; someone was onboard! Ruairí hurriedly turned the bike round and made his way back to the road.

****

Mr Hewitt had come calling with Briege, only two days before, asking her to remove herself and - what was it he had called her home? - "that floating rubbish skip!" The sheer nerve of the man! Briege had tried to reason with Hewitt before bidding him good day. She could now see the funny side of their altercation. She'd been sponging down the boat's windows and was in the process of throwing a bucket of water over them to rinse off the remaining suds when, from nowhere, the breeze had picked up, showering the man with spray as he came up to her. *That's what he gets for his cheek*, she thought.

The article that the Englishman had written for the Gazette was a complete tissue of lies. To say that she had broken the council's bye-laws by being there and paying no fees was nonsense; Briege Geels had never owed money to anyone in her life. She had arrived in Ireland without expectations; peace of mind was all she wanted. She would be keeping herself to herself from here on in.

Whilst listening to a CD of Chopin's nocturnes, she had been wringing out her washing when she accidently nudged the breakfast dishes, causing them to slide into the sink. Looking out of the window, she saw a young boy with a bike. Was he casing the place to break in later with his friends? Taking the laundry basket, Briege made her way on deck, the boy departing as suddenly as he had appeared.

Having finished the chore, Briege went back down below and over to where her old black Bechstein piano sat against the wall. Sitting down, she lifted the lid and began playing Debussy's *Suite Bergamasque*. The instrument seemed to take on a mind of its own, and fleeting memories of when she and her husband Johan used to play duets together came flooding back. The keys were being driven harder now as she recalled that day when her world changed forever.

****

The rain clouds were getting closer and closer as Ruairí pushed his new bike faster than he really should. But now, as if by magic, they were one, boy and machine. His legs began to hurt but he was unable to ease the pace, such was the rush he was experiencing. Old Mrs Murphy, who ran a bed and breakfast, quickly stepped back to the safety of her gate as Ruairí hurtled past her. In his mind's eye, his fans were back, in their thousands, cheering him on to the end of the race.

The next time it would be Cork, he promised himself as he wheeled the bike into the barn, unsettling the piglets. Patrick followed him in.

"Well, is it as good as it looks, Ruairí?"

"It's brill, Dad," he answered, unsure whether it was wise to tell him how fast he had been riding. "It's very speedy but I was careful, and the gears are a great help on the hills. Would you get your old racing bike fixed up, Dad? We could go out as a tag team, relay one another. Please, will you?"

"I'm a little too old for relays, but I could do with the exercise. Aye, I'll get my bike out soon and we'll go for a run. Best get yourself in, your nana's been looking for you," said Patrick, as he put meal in the pigs' feeding trough.

****

"So, you finally decided to come back!" said his mother playfully, as she set his plate in front of him. "Ach, Ruairí, you're all sweaty! It's into the tub with you after dinner, young man. We can't have Father Moloney thinking we never wash! Where did you go?"

Ruairí toyed with his food while he decided if he should make up a little white lie or casually mention his excursion to the lough and the impressive boat that was moored there.

"I went for a bit of a run and ended up at Coolbawn Quay," he said, as if he had arrived there by chance.

"What brought you there?" asked Patrick, having returned from the barn.

"I don't know.... it was a good bit of road to try the Raleigh out on, I suppose," he replied, attempting to create a grown-up statement.

"You're such a fibber, Ruairí Delaney. You were probably listening to Peggy and me as you sat on the stairs, like you usually do!" laughed Maeve.

"Don't be going down there again, it's too far away to be on your own. Do you hear me?" ordered Kathleen sternly.

"What's the boat like?" asked Maeve, her curiosity getting the better of her.

"Maeve!"

"At least let's hear from our Ruairí what all the fuss is about, Kathleen. Go on, pet."

"It's the biggest boat you ever did see, Nana. It's so long and wide you could put a truck in it! It's called *The Johan*. Mr Hewitt's boat looks like a dinghy next to it."

"And was there anyone onboard?"

"A lady came out just as I was leaving."

"What did she look like?"

"Mum, please let Ruairí eat his dinner before it gets cold. It's been a long week and he's bound to be dead beat. Into the bath with you after this and then straight to bed, Ruairí," his father ordered sharply.

Ruairí finished his meal in silence and then hurried off. He knew his parents were displeased and the last thing he wanted was to be grounded.

"Maeve, I must ask that you don't encourage Ruairí; Coolbawn is no place for a child to be out on his own. With the motley bunch of social misfits and degenerates that are running around, anything could have happened to him!" said Kathleen, when her son had left the room.

"What's all this about, Kathleen? I was only asking!"

"If he gets it into his head that there's a story to be told, he'll never be away from the place. I want to see him grow to be a man, not riding the roads unaccompanied."

"I'd best be going now," said the old woman, rising quickly to her feet and snatching her coat, reeling from her daughter-in-law's outburst. "We're all done in and I'm sure that a decent night's sleep will do us good."

****

Kneeling on his ottoman, Ruairí - oblivious to the harsh words being spoken - looked out over the fields, as he often did when trying to figure something out. The Dutchwoman seemed to have a sad face, although he couldn't be sure for there had been little time to study her properly. From what he could remember, she was tall and thin, with beautiful brown hair. Maybe she wasn't sad but ill-tempered, like Master Rankin, or Mr Hewitt.

He would talk it over with his friends on Monday, along with his holiday. He had almost forgotten about Cork. How had he managed to get himself into so much trouble after his recent adventure? Ruairí's thoughts returned to the Dutch barge, swaying gently at its moorings. When his parents had calmed down, he would arrange to bring the whole gang out to see it.

CHAPTER TEN

"I've said this once and I'll say it again: God wants us to do His work. Look around you; is there someone who needs help? Even if it is just a few kind words, it would make such a difference, such a difference to their lives," said Father Moloney as he gave his Sunday sermon. "There is a lady who has decided to put down roots amongst us, at beautiful Coolbawn Quay. Ah, Coolbawn, many's the summer did I go swimming at that very spot in my younger days. But there are those who oppose her being here. This is 1987, for pity's sake! Are we not free to travel and make a new home where we will? Did Jesus not reach out to the leper and heal the poor man? What has this woman done to deserve being hauled over the coals in the Birr Gazette? We must demonstrate tolerance; tolerance is the one thing society needs if we are to live together. Now, let us stand. I believe in one God, the Father almighty…."

Ruairí looked up at his mother, who gave him an *I don't want to hear another word about Father Moloney being boring* look, before joining in with the Creed. Nana - having driven herself to church - had said little this morning, choosing to speak only with his father and her friends. What was so wrong with Coolbawn Quay all of a sudden? He had been down there many times before, even bringing parcels to his nana. One week at the quay and this woman seemed to have caused trouble for everyone. Perhaps Mr Hewitt knew something that the rest of them didn't.

Ruairí walked out to the car park, where his friends waited as their parents talked with other members of the congregation.

"Hi, Ruairí, what's wrong with you today, were you not in Cork all week with all the top racers?" asked Aidan, scraping some gravel with his shoe.

"Yeah, I saw it on the telly. You must have had a blast!" added Donal, who was dressed in an ill-fitting pinstriped suit, his unruly hair in urgent need of taming by the barber.

Rather than get into more trouble for even raising the topic of the barge, Ruairí began to tell his friends all about the race.

"And you actually got to meet Stephen Roche, or did you just see him as he passed by?" Donal enquired.

"I'll have you know that he shook my hand!" answered Ruairí, offended that his friend would doubt him.

"Anybody could say that when no one was there to see it," countered Donal. "Sure, people tell tall tales every day; didn't my dad meet Elvis when he came to Dublin!"

"Did he, Donal? You never said," queried Aidan, with some interest.

"I'm just kidding, you chump. Did you really meet Roche? And what about Kelly? You've been quiet about him, Ruairí."

"If that's all you pair want to do, joke about and call me a liar, well, sod the lot of you. I'm going!" replied Ruairí indignantly.

With that, he turned and walked over to his parent's car. This day was going steadily downhill. First it was his mam; her mood had not lifted from last night and Nana was steering well clear of her. To cap it all, now his friends were set to mock him, rather than hearing about the exhilarating time he had spent in Cork.

****

On the way back to Ballinderry, the only sound came from the radio, with Boxcar Willie singing that he would always be a railroad hobo. To Ruairí, it seemed to be an idyllic life, going where you wanted and leaving when you'd had your fill.

He couldn't wait to change out of his Sunday clothes and go to Gurthalougha Forest. He would take the Grifter as he didn't want to risk damaging his new racer on the uneven ground. It was a dry, overcast day, and he figured that he could get out of the house for at least two hours before dinner was served. There would definitely be one less plate on the table this week; there was no way his nana would be having dinner with them, given her mood in church.

****

Ruairí found his father setting out the Sunday papers on the stand, ready for people returning from Mass.

"Can I go to the treehouse for a while, Dad?" he asked.

"Oh, you're already changed! Alright so, but take your watch with you and be back at one on the dot. Your mother isn't feeling well so don't annoy her by being late," he replied.

"Dad."

"Yes?"

"Is something the matter?"

"What do you mean, son?"

"No one was talking this morning."

"Oh, I wouldn't worry about that. When there are two headstrong women in one house, there will always be a bit of who knows best. Your mam isn't herself at present, the holiday took it out of her. As for your nana, she's grand. She likes to keep a hand on things and sometimes it gets her in trouble. Now, away with you before it's too late and don't forget your watch; one o'clock, do you hear me?"

"Yes, one o'clock," said Ruairí as he went upstairs, stopping to admire the signed racing cap sitting on his dresser.

Adults were so difficult to understand, thought Ruairí, as he journeyed along the empty road where yellow tufts of grass adorned the ditches. Why couldn't Mam tell him she was feeling unwell? He would have tried extra hard to keep out of mischief. It was tricky being eleven, with everyone assuming you could read their minds. He had simply gone for a run, and ended up at an old barge. Perhaps he had pushed his luck, just a little. Everyone - even his friends - was on his case today.

****

As Ruairí neared his destination, an old farmer passed by in his tractor, pipe in mouth, nodding like a little toy dog on the back shelf of a car. Leaning the Grifter against a bush, he climbed into the treehouse by way of a makeshift ladder. He was startled to find Oisín Halloran sitting there, drinking from a can of Irn-Bru. Wearing a new ensemble of jeans, shirt and jumper, with a grey zip-up bomber jacket, Ruairí thought he looked more like his old self again.

"Hi, Oisín," said Ruairí, finding his voice, "are you back?"

Oisín looked out over the fields, a little uncomfortable. He was sure that everybody would know by now what had been happening to him.

"I was hoping you'd turn up here, Ruairí. Listen, I'm sorry for losing the head with you. I shouldn't have dropped you."

"It's cool, Oisín, I know things have been hard for you lately."

"Have any of the others spoken about it.... you know, laughed at me? Probably that headbin, Donal?"

"I wouldn't worry about him, he has trouble lacing his shoes never mind remembering what happened yesterday. Aidan was asking about you. I suppose everybody has. You've had a miserable time of it, Oisín. Are you coming back to school?"

"Yes, tomorrow. Dad's moved out, so me and Mam are back home again. Aunt Jacinta's going to call round now and again to make sure we're okay. Someone said you were in Cork, at the racing; how was it?"

Ruairí began to smile. Finally, somebody was genuinely interested in what had happened! He could tell Oisín how he had met his hero and not be ridiculed. They talked for nearly an hour before Ruairí had to go; he wasn't about to get into any more bother for one day.

****

"We were nearly giving up on you, young man," said Maeve, as she drained the peas, whilst Kathleen made gravy and Patrick carved the roast.

Ruairí stood there in total confusion. Only this morning they had used separate cars. Nana had kept to her friends during Mass, and Mam would have scowled at anyone who looked at her crooked. He thanked God for making the grown-ups see sense.

Ruairí ate his meal in silence, not wanting to say the wrong thing. He smiled to himself at the thought of Oisín being back in school. After dinner, he brushed his teeth and changed into camouflage-print pyjamas. Flopping onto his bed, he opened Roald Dahl's *Boy* at the page where he had left off. He always chuckled at the stories in the book, especially the one about the prank played on Mrs Pratchett.

From such a disappointing morning to now, Ruairí didn't care if it poured out of the heavens. Everyone was laughing and talking, and the big oak tree in the garden seemed to be tapping on the window in merriment. As a treat, he put on the big fellow's cap and continued to read his book. Ruairí looked up as he heard a floorboard creak on the landing. The door handle turned, and Kathleen tiptoed in.

"Any room for one more?" she asked.

"Only if you like dead mice and gobstoppers!"

Kathleen gave Ruairí a cuddle.

"Am I still your favourite Mam?"

"Um," he replied, enjoying the affection.

"I'm sorry for being so grumpy with you today. I was feeling a little poorly. How was the treehouse; did you have fun on your own?"

"Oisín was there when I arrived."

"Was he? And how's he doing?"

"He and his mam are back at their old house. His dad doesn't live there anymore."

"The poor wee mite, he's had it tough. You don't know when you're well-off, mister," joked Kathleen as she tickled him, sending him into fits of laughter.

"Mam, I'm trying to read my book!" he said in between giggles as he squirmed around on the bed.

"Well, make sure you come down to the kitchen in half an hour. There's apple tart and custard for you when you've made some room in that belly of yours," she said giving his tummy a gentle prod, before placing a kiss on his forehead.

As his mother left the room to continue ironing his uniform, Ruairí could still smell her perfume on his bedclothes. Setting down the book, he put his face to the pillow and inhaled deeply. He would always remember that scent.

CHAPTER ELEVEN

The place was in an uproar. Kathleen had slept in due to the holiday and, consequently, so had everyone else in the Delaney household.

"Ruairí, I won't call you again, you'll be late!" shouted Patrick as he made himself bacon and eggs while Kathleen prepared her son's lunch.

Ruairí eventually appeared at the kitchen door, rubbing sleep from his eyes. His mother walked over to him and straightened his tie.

"Sit down and eat your Weetabix, it won't be long before the bus will be here. Why can't you get up when you're called? Patrick, when are you going to the cash and carry? Is it after you help Brendan?"

"We'll drop off the cattle from the trailer and load the jeep up with what's been ordered. They got the fax yesterday, so it should be sitting ready."

"As long as it gets here around noon. Any later and the customers will assume that we haven't paid our bills!"

Patrick planted a big bacon and egg kiss on his wife's cheek as he stood eating his breakfast.

"You're disgusting," she said with a smile, closing Ruairí's lunchbox.

"Don't be panicking, they'll have the order made up. Two hours will do us at the sale yard and then we'll call by the wholesalers. Sit yourself down, Kathleen, and have your breakfast. Ruairí, shake a leg, you've quarter of an hour to get the bus or you'll be going in Brendan's trailer!"

"I'm ready, I'm just packing my lunchbox," he replied, quickly zipping up the bag.

"Come here, you," said Kathleen. "Look at that hair, we can't have you going out like that."

"But that's the style now, Mam!" he tried to explain, his hair sitting like an unkempt haystack until she brushed it into a side parting.

"Away with you now. Watch the roads and behave yourself!"

As the bus pulled up, Ruairí could see Oisín sitting near the back. At least he had someone to chat with before Donal got on: he would start talking about fishing or the size of elephants' brains.

****

"What's with that bullock today, Brendan? He's very skittish," Patrick commented as they started transferring the cattle from the pen and onto the trailer.

"I don't know, Patrick. Maybe they were fooling about during the night and he took a knock. Just keep an eye on him for now. When the hammer drops in the ring, he'll be someone else's problem."

The two men herded the six bullocks on board and closed the loading ramp. The livestock, unsettled, kicked and rocked the trailer in protest.

"What do you expect to get for them, Brendan; it's a bit early for letting them go, is it not?"

"The French are about to flood the market with cheap meat, having lost a big contract with Russia."

"Is that so?"

"Aye, they caught two KGB agents trying to break into the Dutch Embassy in Paris and the pair were expelled. So now the Russians are blocking French imports, including beef. They'll subsidise their own market, leaving the wholesale price in free fall," explained Brendan.

"Sounds like a bit of a gamble but you may as well go for it," said Patrick, opening the jeep's window for some fresh air as they drove off.

"I'd rather sell at today's prices. Just you wait, next week or the week after will prove me right."

On their arrival at the sale yard in Birr, the men were directed over to an unloading pen, into which Brendan reversed the jeep and trailer. The livestock had still not settled and were very agitated, kicking about inside. The trailer loading ramp was lowered and the bullocks hesitantly began leaving, all but the moody animal. It stood immobile.

"I'll go and give him a poke with the cane, send him on his way," suggested Patrick.

"Just watch him, Patrick, he probably won't budge. He's just as cantankerous as his mother."

Patrick went around to the trailer's side door. Opening the latch, he reached in with a blackthorn herding stick to hasten the animal's departure.

****

Master Rankin was writing mathematical formulae on the whiteboard when Headmaster Finlay entered the room and spoke with him, nodding at Ruairí as he did so. For the life of him, Ruairí couldn't recollect doing anything that would have resulted in the head coming to see him. Perhaps it was someone else who was in bother.

Master Rankin looked in Ruairí's direction.

"Ruairí Delaney, put your books away and bring your bag with you, please."

Now he was really worried. Take his bag with him? That's what happened to his friends when they were caught fighting in the toilets. He hadn't been fighting with anyone.

"Ruairí, please come with me," said the headmaster as he led him from the room.

"But I haven't done anything wrong, Master Finlay!"

"I know that, Ruairí, your grandmother has come to collect you."

"Why? Has something happened?"

"It's best that she speaks with you," said the man, opening the door to his office.

Maeve sat there, her handbag on her lap, dabbing her eyes with a soggy handkerchief. Ruairí knew instinctively that something terrible must have taken place. She put down her bag and took him in her arms, weeping uncontrollably, holding him so tight he could barely breathe.

"What's wrong, Nana, why are you crying?"

Letting go of Ruairí, Maeve composed herself and lifted her bag.

"Thanks for your help, Mr Finlay, but we need to be on our way now."

"Can I order you a taxi, Mrs Delaney? Or I could ask a member of staff to drive you both home?"

"My car's outside, but thank you nonetheless."

And with this, Maeve led her grandson out to the car park.

****

As Ruairí got into the car, he felt more scared than he had ever been in his whole life. He had never seen his grandmother like this before and her reticence had unnerved him.

"Nana, what's the matter?" he asked. "Please, tell me!"

"There's been an accident…. your mam will tell you everything when we get back," said Maeve. "Put your seat belt on, Ruairí, there's a good lad."

****

As Maeve drove past the shop, Ruairí noticed that the store was in darkness, which was strange for this time of day. There was a Garda car parked round the back. He went in and started to make his way upstairs, pausing halfway when hearing an unknown female voice which seemed to be coming from the sitting room. Ruairí tried to make sense of what she was saying, that it had been a freak accident and that the ambulance crew had tried their best. He had no idea what the lady could be talking about.

Ruairí entered the room, finding his mother there along with Father Moloney and two Gardaí. His bag dropped to the floor.

"Mam, what's happened, why are all these people here?"

Kathleen reached out to her son and pulled him close.

"Ruairí, there's been an accident, one of Brendan O'Riordan's…."

Ruairí let out a scream that took everyone by surprise. Struggling to free himself, he continued to scream, the sound reverberating around the room. Kathleen held him tightly but Ruairí was inconsolable; something told him that Father Moloney's angels had made an appearance and his dad would never be coming home again.

****

"It's a sad state of affairs, Doctor, nothing ever prepares you for it," said Maeve, quietly closing Ruairí's bedroom door, her eyes red from crying.

"I'm so sorry for your loss, Maeve, there's nothing I can say or do to make things any better. I would ask you to look in on Ruairí from time to time. This has shaken him to the core. And where's Kathleen? I need to examine her also."

“She’s in the kitchen. To tell you the truth, I’m worried about her.”

Doctor Walsh found Kathleen standing at the sink, her face buried deep in one of Patrick’s white shirts that she had taken from the wardrobe.

“I’m grand,” she said, in reply to his enquiry regarding her wellbeing. “I must get this ready; Patrick will need something to wear when he comes home.”

“Enough,” said the man, in a gentle but firm voice. He led her to the bedroom, with Maeve in tow, and sat her down to check her blood pressure.

“Kathleen, you’re worn out. You must rest!”

“Ruairí needs me and there are arrangements to be made, I’ve no time for resting!”

“You have to be strong for Ruairí now,” he argued, persuading her to lie down for a few hours.

****

“Where’s Kathleen?” asked Father Moloney, on Maeve’s return.

“She’s asleep, Father.”

“And you? This can’t be easy, burying your son.”

“I’ll go on. Patrick should have been the one burying me, but that won’t happen now. Shall I make you some tea? I’m putting the kettle on, for this will be a long night.”

****

Maeve filled the kettle and switched it on, wiping the draining board down with a cloth. She could not fully comprehend what had taken place that morning. Hot tears filled her eyes once more, and her throat constricted at the realisation that Patrick wasn't coming back. What made it harder was that she had not even had the chance to say goodbye to her son, all over the head of that Brendan O'Riordan, as - wanting to make an early start - Patrick had left the store before her arrival. She was entirely convinced who was to blame for all of this. Like his father before him, O'Riordan was always taking short cuts, just to claw in those few extra punts, regardless of who paid the price. *God forgive me, but may he rot in hell!* whispered Maeve as she set out the cups on a tray.

****

Kathleen rose early the next morning, feeling slightly groggy until she remembered the events of yesterday. Burying her face in the pillow, she tried to subdue the sounds of her overwhelming agony, recounting those last few hours with her husband before he left their lives forever. Some inner force compelled her to get up. Quickly putting on a touch of concealer to hide the dark circles under her eyes, she went straight to Ruairí's room. She let out a sigh of relief; she'd had a terrifying dream that both Patrick and Ruairí had been taken from her. Lying on the bed with her son, she gently cradled him as when he was a newborn until sleep stole over her once again.

Maeve went into the room a little later, and placed a quilt over her daughter-in-law. There was a slight tinge of jealousy, but only for a second, that at least Kathleen still had her son while she did not. Closing the door, she blessed herself and asked God's forgiveness for having such a selfish thought.

Father Moloney had stopped over for the night, ensuring that the fire remained lit, and praying for everyone. Maeve fell into fits of deep sleep, interspersed with waking and sobbing bitterly.

The grey light of dawn trickled through the gaps in the curtains and Maeve rose to face the day ahead. As she made for the kitchen, she noticed Father Moloney resting an arm on the sitting room mantelpiece, smoking a cigarette. The old lady went about her business silently so as not to disturb him. The poor man had not even taken a nap and must surely be exhausted, just like her.

Lord, please give me strength to go on, she petitioned silently, rubbing an old brass crucifix which hung on the wall above the fridge.

CHAPTER TWELVE

When Ruairí opened his eyes, his thoughts returned to the previous evening. As he slept, his mind had been full of dragons and horned demons, fighting the bit out at Gurthalougha. He dreamt they were trying to drag his father away. Using a wooden sword that he had carved, he fought valiantly until they overpowered him and his dad disappeared into the mist. Turning, he saw his mother asleep, the quilt draped over her, and the previous day came flooding back with clarity. In a blind panic, he shook Kathleen hard, the shock causing her to wake with a jolt.

"My poor lamb, how are you today?" she enquired, fighting back her emotions.

Tears spilling down his cheeks, Ruairí tried in vain to answer but no sound came forth.

"Ruairí, speak to me, tell me what's wrong!" implored his mother.

Maeve came to the door, having heard her daughter-in-law's raised voice.

"He's been knocked for six, Kathleen," said the old woman, as she felt Ruairí's forehead to check for a fever.

"Maeve, stay here with him, I'm going to ring the doctor," whispered Kathleen, unsure of what else to do.

"I can tell you one thing, he's going to need a lot of love and patience," said Maeve, as she looked at her grandson. "You can't turn grief off like a light switch. All we can do is be there for the lad."

Kathleen went to make the call, her hand shaking as she picked up the receiver. With Doctor Walsh promising to drop by, she returned to help Ruairí get dressed. People would soon be coming by to offer their condolences and she wanted him to look his best.

****

Ruairí stood in the corner of the kitchen with his racing cap on, watching the comings and goings. Why had Brendan O'Riordan needed someone to go with him to the stupid cattle market in the first place? Nana was right, she'd said that he was big enough and ugly enough to look after a few cows on his own, so why hadn't he? And why, after all of Father Moloney's talk about being good, had God chosen to take such a good person as his dad away?

Racked with sobs, his mother came running to comfort him, with little success. It was to be this way during the funeral Mass, Ruairí holding onto his father's coffin, trying to get the words out that God was cruel for leaving him alone, as was Father Moloney, for telling lies that God takes care of everyone.

Kathleen stayed close to her son when the mourners had finally dispersed and they were on their own. Maeve's sister was coming to stay with her at the cottage for a while, but Patrick had been Maeve's only living bond to her husband and his death had left a void nothing could fill.

****

Kathleen had had another restless night; the bed was devoid of any heat now that her partner had been taken from her. Their room, once full of laughter, with Ruairí at three years old jumping up and down on them both, was but a hollow shell. Going into the bathroom, she stared at her reflection in the mirror. *All those years together and now you're gone, gone too soon*, she said to herself as she gently wept.

Ruairí woke from another one of his nightmares. He had been in the treehouse, watching through the darkness while ghouls pranced around wildly below him. He kept squirting them with the water pistol until they eventually ran away, hissing and laughing. Sitting up in bed, he saw the faint yellow glow of the landing light from beneath his door and, throwing back the blankets, ran screaming for his father.

On hearing her son's cries, Kathleen dropped the glass she had been drinking from onto the tiled floor, where it landed with a deafening crash. As she turned, the door opened and Ruairí dashed in. Gathering him into her arms, she carried him back to bed, trying to make him see that his dad was at peace.

"I know you're hurting, Ruairí. So am I, but Daddy's with the angels now and he's looking down on us." Putting his hand on her chest, she added, "He'll always be in our hearts, that's why we must be strong."

"Why couldn't Brendan O'Riordan look after his own smelly cows? Dad would still be here!"

"Brendan had been your father's best friend since they were wee mites. He didn't mean for this to happen and he's as sad as the rest of us," said Kathleen, holding back her tears.

"His stupid animal killed my dad! I hate him, I hate him and his flipping farm! I never want to see him again!"

"Please, Ruairí, don't speak ill of Brendan, nobody is to blame. It was just an accident."

"I don't care. I hate animals and I hate Brendan O'Riordan and his whole family!" he yelled.

Ruairí turned his back on her, staring unseeingly at the window as dawn began to break.

"You're all I have left, pet," she whispered softly, putting her arms around him and Ruairí wept until exhaustion overcame him.

Having finally got him to sleep, she rose and gently closed the door behind her. It had made her feel a little better that Ruairí was talking again, but his anguish was palpable and Dr Walsh had intimated that he might require counselling.

****

Two weeks had passed. Ruairí's frame of mind had improved somewhat and he no longer cried for his father, spending most of his days out on the bike. Aidan seemed to be the only person he wanted to talk to.

"That's yours, Kathleen," said Maeve as she brought their teas to the shop counter. "You're going to have to let go of him, you know."

"I do know, Maeve, it's just the thought of it. He's all I have now but something's changed inside him."

"Did you really expect the lad to come out of this unscathed?"

Kathleen took a tissue from her pocket as the tears came without warning.

"I'm sorry for upsetting you, pet. I know what you're saying, and I've noticed it in him myself. He's hurting and only time will heal such a wound. Get him back out amongst his friends, it's the best medicine there is."

Deep down, Kathleen knew that Ruairí needed to return to school. It would help everyone resume something approximating a normal life.

"You're right, Maeve, I'm being too overprotective. On Monday, he's going back to Terryglass. Where is he anyway? The last I saw of him, he was in his room."

"He's tinkering with his racing bike in the store. Woe betide anything happening to that, given the care he takes of it."

****

Using the valet kit his father had bought for him in Cork, Ruairí began to wipe down the frame of the bike. His parents had agreed that he could keep it in the storeroom to prevent it from rusting in the barn. As he looked about, there was not a cobweb in sight. He had gone around, systematically eradicating every single one. The place was so spotless that even the wolf spiders had vacated the premises.

Nana had sat him down to talk about how they should try to get by without Patrick now that he was no longer there. Ruairí tried hard to control himself, but when she spoke of how it had been God's will and that, one day, they would all be together again in heaven, he became irate. Mr Rankin often said that God was the shepherd who protected His flock. Why was his dad so different from all the other dads, why didn't God protect him? Nana had no answers to give, not that his friends would be of any more help. They would ask him how he was, or if he was feeling better, when all he really wanted was to get on his bike and pedal far away until he found a place where nobody could interrogate him. That's when he'd be feeling better.

The shop doorbell chimed. It was too early for the postman. *Must be a customer*, thought Ruairí, busily applying more polish to his cloth.

****

"Morning," said Maeve as a woman entered the store, carrying an oversized hessian shopping bag. She was around forty years of age, of average height and build with short, brown hair.

"Hello," she replied as she walked on and began picking items off the shelves.

"Who's that?" whispered Kathleen, setting their cups under the counter.

"It could only be the Dutchwoman! She seems to have kept to herself since she got here."

"Don't you be nosing into her business, Maeve, she might become a regular customer."

"And would I do that, Kathleen?"

"Of course you would; you and your old biddies want to know everybody's goings on. Sure, how would the tabloids survive without you all?"

It was the first time the pair had smiled in weeks, let alone bantered with one other.

The woman approached the counter and set her basket of groceries down.

"Is this everything?" asked Kathleen as she packed the lady's bag.

In her Dutch accent, she acknowledged that they were her purchases for now.

"That will be twenty-two punts forty, please," said Maeve, having rung the order through the cash register.

The woman handed over the exact money and closed her purse. Lifting her shopping, she turned to leave.

"I take it you're not from around these parts?" Maeve blurted out, unable to contain her curiosity; Kathleen gave her a kick on the shin for her lack of social graces.

"I am from Rotterdam…. and now, if you don't mind, I need to be on my way. Good day to you both."

With this, she left the store, hopped on her bike and rode off.

"I told you not to ask her anything, she probably won't come back now," scolded Kathleen.

"Ach, sure it was an innocent question anybody would have asked. There's no helping someone that uptight."

Maeve tutted and, shaking her head, took the cups upstairs to put on another brew. Kathleen was completely unaware that her mother-in-law had a fair idea as to the Dutchwoman's origins but, for now, Maeve had resolved to keep it to herself.

****

On hearing the woman's voice, Ruairí had stopped what he was doing and froze. He thought she had called to complain about him hanging around her boat, even though that was a while ago now. Cautiously peering round the partially opened door, he watched her as she perused the merchandise. The woman seemed a sullen looking type. Nevertheless, he was intrigued by her accent, which was so exotic to him.

CHAPTER THIRTEEN

Ruairí waved to his mother and got on the bus, choosing a seat near the middle. The rowdies would board later and head straight for the rear, where the banter and mischief-making took place. Ruairí wanted none of it. His only desire was to be left alone so that he could get the day over with. The bus came to a halt a couple of miles away and a sleepy-looking Aidan clambered on board.

"How's it going, Ruairí?" he enquired, setting his bag down on the floor in front of him.

"What's it to you?"

"I was only asking!"

"Well, don't."

"I'm just trying to…."

"Shut up, would you!" yelled Ruairí, abruptly ending the conversation. He wasn't ready to go back to school and he had told his mam so, but she was having none of it. Why did grown-ups never listen?

****

At morning assembly, a Mass was said for Patrick Delaney. Ruairí sat through it as though enduring a thousand lashes, unable to avoid the sympathetic looks from teachers and pupils alike. He hoped that, after today, he would be left in peace. They really had no idea what it was like for him at home. Every room he went into, his father was there in some form. His LPs, his books, his shaving kit, and the old racing bike in the barn: all sharp reminders of Ruairí's loss.

"Ruairí, may I speak with you in my office?" requested Headmaster Finlay.

Ruairí was filled with a sudden dread, guessing that there would be a sermon given once the door was closed.

"Now, Ruairí, I'm not going to say I understand what you're going through because I don't, I couldn't even begin to. I would just like you to know that, if you ever need to talk, my door is always open."

Ruairí gazed out of the window, contemplating whether to jump through it and be gone, to be anywhere but here.

"Did you hear me, Ruairí?"

"Yes, sir, I'm fine but thank you anyway."

"That's all I wanted to say. It's good to have you back. Run along now, class will have started."

Ruairí lifted his bag and headed off. It could have been worse. Finlay wasn't always so soft when you were called to his office. As he took his seat, Donal shook his shoulder, telling him he would be alright. Ruairí had a mind to get back up and thump him but thought better of it. It was probably Donal's innocuous way of empathising with him.

At breaktime, Ruairí shuffled aimlessly around the playground, preferring to be on his own. Sensing this, Aidan had chosen to mingle with his other pals instead.

“Life’s a bowl of crap,” said Oisín Halloran, edging his way towards him.

“Oisín.”

“I’ll go if you want.”

Ruairí shrugged his shoulders, stopping at the boundary fence.

“Forget about Donnelly and the rest of them. Pull the shutters down and just look after yourself,” said Oisín, kicking at the gravel below his foot.

“Whatever…. I don’t care anymore.”

Ruairí studied Oisín’s face, taking a long, hard look at him.

“What was your dad really like, Oisín?”

“Too fond of the bottle, and always knocking me and Mam about. The only peace we had was when he was drunk and asleep, or out of the house,” said Oisín, lowering his head.

Taken aback, Ruairí didn’t know what to say.

“He’s gone now and we never want to set eyes on him again. I always wanted my dad to be more like yours. I was so jealous when you came in on a Monday morning and told us all about your weekends with him.”

Ruairí looked at Oisín in astonishment. Until now, he had taken it for granted that every father and son spent time together.

“Do you fancy heading out some evening on the bikes?” asked Oisín.

“I don’t know…. Mam needs me at home,” replied Ruairí; he had never hung out with Oisín on his own before and wasn’t sure if it was a good idea.

The bell rang, calling them back to their English lesson. As the pair walked down the corridor, Ruairí thought about what Oisín had just said. All these years they had spent together, and he really knew very little about him.

****

Briege Geels was on deck, watering the seedlings she had planted some weeks earlier. She was hoping for a bumper crop of salad leaves for the summer, if the insects didn't ruin them first. Returning to her deckchair, she viewed Lough Derg and its expanse; it was an idyllic place to live.

Whilst the petty-minded protest about her barge being moored at Coolbawn Quay had come to an end, the behaviour of some of the yacht owners still left a lot to be desired. Twice they had disconnected her electric, until she involved An Garda Síochána. But, for now, she could tolerate their dirty looks; she wouldn't be uprooting herself again for anyone.

She began to make a list of provisions she was running low on. Having no car and with an almost non-existent bus service, the nearest place was Delaney's store in Ballinderry. Briege had read about the tragic accident in the local paper. The young boy.... she knew he was watching when she had first called at the store as his shadow had given him away. God only knew what he was going through.

Briege thought back to those carefree days spent growing up in Holland, and that accidental meeting with Johan as they both huddled under a greengrocer's shop awning from the rain. Once married, they had bought an old barge and renovated it, making Rotterdam their home. Unable to have children, their own company sufficed, and they had twenty blissful years together before life was changed irrevocably.

Now Briege had had enough of her adopted homeland. After many frantic phone calls and meetings with engineers, she succeeded in having her entire belongings shipped over to Ireland, to Coolbawn.

****

"How was your day, Ruairí?" asked his mother as she wrote down items she needed to stock up on.

"Headmaster Finlay had me in for a lecture."

Kathleen stopped what she was doing and looked up from her writing.

"What did he want? Is everything okay?"

"He just said that I could always speak to him if I needed to."

"That was kind of him."

"I don't need to speak to anyone, Dad's dead and talking won't bring him back!"

"That's a dreadful thing to say about the man who raised you for the past eleven years. Don't imagine for one minute that you can shut him out of our lives!"

The words rolled off her lips before she could take them back, sending Ruairí bolting up the stairs and into his bedroom. He had heard enough for one day. Everyone was wrong, they all wanted to meddle in something that nobody could fix. Spotting his box of *Road Wheels* on the floor, he took them one by one and tore them to shreds.

When Kathleen opened the bedroom door, she was dismayed to see the ruined stack of paper on the floor and her son kneeling on the ottoman, elbows on the windowsill.

"Ruairí, what have you done to your lovely magazines? Your father and I never brought you up to behave like this!"

"Stop talking like he's still here. They're old, and I've read them all. The pigs can bed on them," he replied coldly, still with his back to her.

"Don't you dare speak to me in that tone, Ruairí Delaney, I want this mess cleaned up right away! Your tea's nearly ready although you don't deserve it, so you'd best get busy!" yelled his mother before storming out of the room.

****

"What's wrong now?" asked Maeve, counting out a customer's change.

"I don't know what to do with him, Maeve, I'm barely holding myself together. He's trying to shut his father out of his life," she replied as the shop door closed.

"I told you he's going to need a lot of patience. Giving off to him won't solve things."

"He's just gone mad and ripped up all of those cycling magazines Patrick gave him. They were beyond repair, in a heap on the floor, when I went in."

"Now that's just too much!" exclaimed Maeve, shaking her head in disbelief. "I'll be having words with him!"

"Leave him be, Maeve. Let him have his tea and toast, and hopefully he'll be in a better mood by then but, if he thinks he's getting away with this, he's got another think coming!"

"Do you want me to stay over, Kathleen? I could help out. After all, it's only me padding about in that little cottage of mine."

Kathleen had only heard snippets of Maeve's words, her mind being focused on her son and his recent behaviour. But the thought of her as a permanent fixture was something she couldn't handle. Having Maeve in the shop was one thing, living with her was another.

"I'll be fine, Maeve. Ruairí and I need to work this out on our own. I'm away to make his tea. Thank you for your kind offer," said Kathleen, touching the old woman's arm affectionately.

****

On his hands and knees, Ruairí was bitterly regretting the irreparable damage he had caused to his treasured collection. His father used to enjoy them as much as he did. Why had he done such a thing and, worse still, why had he been so horrible to his mother? Nana was bound to have heard all about it by now, and she would have something to say regarding his behaviour! He hurriedly rolled their remains into a ball, crept downstairs and out to the back yard where he threw it in the bin. By the time Ruairí got to the kitchen, his tea was already on the table.

Kathleen glanced at him and then carried on mashing potatoes for the shepherd's pie she was making.

"Do you have much homework?"

"English, Maths and Geography," he replied, through a mouthful of toast.

"Well, make a start on it while the dinner's cooking and I'll be in to help you shortly," said his mother curtly.

CHAPTER FOURTEEN

A new month crept in with little fanfare. For the Delaneys, one week rolled into the next. Kathleen remained strong for Ruairí but, deep inside, the hurt and the pain of losing Patrick tore at her like a searing lance. Night time was when she felt at her lowest. She had seriously considered selling the shop, and her husband's farmstead that had been left to him by his late father. But this was Ruairí's home and there was his schooling to take into account, not to mention his friends. And how would Maeve feel if they decided to pull up stakes and go?

It was a fine morning and, leaving her mother-in-law to open the store, Kathleen went for a walk. The trees were in full bloom and the fragrant scent of the hawthorn bushes that lined the road began to lift her mood. For a moment, she felt so alive and she paused to observe a robin redbreast that had settled on an overhanging branch. Kathleen pondered the likelihood of loved ones coming back as robins before the little bird flew off, having been startled by her presence. Glancing at her watch, she saw that it had just turned ten to nine. She ought to get back to the shop, but this was now becoming an unwelcome chore.

****

"I'm a bit disappointed by the standard of your work lately," said Mr Rankin, having asked Ruairí to remain behind.

Ruairí sat impassively, not really caring, much less wanting to be there.

"You must have something to say?" the teacher enquired. "I know things have not been the same since…. well, since the death of your father. It's not been an easy time, I'm sure, for any of you but he would have wanted you to…."

"I don't need you to tell me what he would have wanted, that's my work and if it's not good enough you know what you can do with it!"

Grabbing his schoolbag, Ruairí fled from the classroom. Astonished by his outburst, Mr Rankin called out to him, wondering if he had perhaps been a little insensitive, but Ruairí kept on running, nearly colliding with the caretaker before barging through the main entrance.

Aidan, Liam, Donal, and Oisín were in the schoolyard and spotted Ruairí exiting the building, tailing him as he tried to make his way alone to the other side of the playground. Six weeks he had been back and it was not getting any easier. Everyone was being very kind, but their kindness was suffocating him.

"What did Rankin want, Ruairí?" asked Liam.

"He was droning on about my crappy homework," he replied, looking for a way to escape.

"You'll be fine, sure my dad left school with nothing!" remarked Donal.

"Aye and look what he produced," said Oisín sarcastically, shoving him into a group of girls who began to scream.

“Leave him alone, Oisín,” said Aidan, coming between them. “Put a hand on him again and you’ll get a hiding!”

Oisín just laughed and walked away.

“When are you going to stand up for yourself, Donal? Are you always going to let everyone pick on you?” Aidan asked.

“It was nothing,” argued Donal, trying to shake off the assault as a bit of banter. “Let it go, Aidan, he’s just an eejit like the rest of us.”

The bell rang, signalling the end of morning break and allowing Ruairí to disengage from any further conversation. So what if Oisín had pushed Donal? Aidan always had to be the superhero, leaping in to save the day. Flinging his bag under the table, Ruairí avoided eye contact with Mr Rankin, looking forward to having his lunch alone in the canteen.

****

Maeve had called to collect them for Sunday Mass as Kathleen was feeling unwell and thought it best not to drive. The car seemed to be navigating to the church by itself as she spent more time talking to Kathleen than watching the road.

“I told Alice Brown that she wore too much make-up for a woman her age, but would she listen?.... Charlie McKimmon has been seen out with a new woman and his wife not six months’ dead!”

The stories went on and on. Turn signals, gear changes, waving at someone along the road, all coordinated and still she would find time to occasionally glance in the rear-view mirror at Ruairí.

The church was packed, with everyone in their best Sunday clothes. There had been a missionary priest staying at the parochial house who'd been helping with the weekday services and the visiting of the sick. Ruairí hoped he was still there. The young man came from Sierra Leone and he knew how to deliver a Sunday Mass at the double. Half an hour was his current record. As the entrance bell rang, Father Moloney emerged from the sacristy, surrounded by four altar servers. Ruairí's heart sank.

"This is going to be a long one, Mam," said Ruairí, before his nan nudged him with her elbow, following this with a scornful look that would *turn a crow to stone*, one of her favourite sayings.

With the gospel at an end, the priest began telling the congregation that God would look after those who chose the path of righteousness.

"Those who seek to live their lives against the Father's teachings will be dammed in hell, dammed in hell. You must lead a good life if you want to go to heaven. To be with God and walk in his path will get you to eternity, I cannot emphasise that enough. You young people must accept God into your hearts if you want salvation."

Ruairí sat there confused. He longed to ask his mother if his father had been such a good man, and Ruairí knew he had been, he was always helping people, why had God chosen to take him. Deciding against speaking in case Nana started on him again, he thought back to the religious lessons in school. For the life of him, he still could not comprehend why the greatest man he had ever known had gone, forever.

"My dear people, let us reflect upon the way we live each day. Are our thoughts kind and our deeds honourable, or will they hurt our neighbour? These are questions, honest questions that each and every one of us must ask of ourselves, if we truly love God. Only then will we find the answers we're searching for. Now, let us stand for the Creed."

After Mass, Kathleen and Ruairí went straight to the car. Maeve socialised for a while, nattering with her friends and filling them in on the latest juicy pieces of gossip, gleaned over the course of her working week.

"Mam."

"Yes, pet?" she replied, looking in the mirror of her compact whilst fixing her mascara with a tissue.

"Was Dad a bad man?"

Kathleen quickly turned to face her son.

"Whatever gave you that notion?"

"Father Moloney said that if you lead a good life then God will look after you. Dad left us, so he must have done something that we didn't know about and God found out!"

Kathleen got out of the car and opened the rear door where her son was seated.

"Now, you listen here, Ruairí Delaney. Your father never did a bad thing in his life, ask your nana and she'll tell you that herself. Religion is complicated and sometimes words can be used that give out a different message to what the person really intended. Father Moloney meant that we should be careful about what we say and do, otherwise people's feelings can get hurt. You know rightly your father was the finest man that ever lived," said Kathleen, with a hint of anger in her voice, tears destroying her immaculately-applied mascara.

****

"Ruairí, go and change while I make something for you to eat and, after that, I want you to take yourself out. You're not going to waste the day lounging around here," said Kathleen.

Ruairí relished the opportunity to get away for a while. For some reason, the spirits of 1916 were misbehaving more than usual and the house had become noisier at night than ever before. He had wanted to ask his mother if they could move, but he was anxious not to cause any more upset.

After feasting on a bacon and egg sandwich, and a mug of tea, Ruairí took the Raleigh racing bike from the store and made his way out. He began to fasten the strap of the helmet under his chin and then checked over the controls before setting off.

"Here, take your jacket with you," said Kathleen, hurrying out. "Don't be riding too fast. Remember, there's nothing between you and the road. Be back in an hour! Do you hear?"

"Yes, Mam, but I don't need a jacket!"

"I'm not having you catching a cold and missing school. Off you go now," she insisted, before returning indoors.

"Religion, it's the cause of so much misery in the world!" exclaimed Kathleen, folding her arms disapprovingly.

Maeve, who had been reading a copy of *Ireland's Own*, looked over her glasses inquisitively, trying to follow the reasoning behind the statement.

"What do you mean?" she asked, setting the magazine aside.

"Ruairí has got it into his head that Patrick must have been a bad man and that's why God took him. Father Moloney could be a bit more sensitive about the wording of his sermons!"

"When was all this?"

"This morning, at Mass. Can you tell me when things are supposed to get better, Maeve? One minute Ruairí's settled and then it all kicks off again. How could he ever distrust his own father?" she said, tears flooding her eyes.

"Where is he now?"

"I sent him out on his bike for a while. He's cooped up enough in this bloody place. I wish we were back in Portlaoise!"

Mystified by her daughter-in-law's words, Maeve studied her drained appearance. A sudden thought came to mind, but she decided to keep her own counsel. Following Patrick's death, Maeve had vowed to see her days out behind the store counter so that she could be laid to rest near him. The shop wouldn't be getting sold anytime soon, she would make sure of that.

"Now, Kathleen, you must look after yourself. I'm not as young as I used to be, and I can't be caring for Ruairí and the store if you become poorly. Go and have a lie down and I'll start the dinner. Only God knows how hard it is to go on after losing someone you love."

Maeve was feeling uneasy. She had recently begun to experience a slight tightness in her chest, but she saw little point in making an appointment with Doctor Walsh, the man was rushed off his feet as it was. She was determined to get on with things as best she could. She rubbed Kathleen's shoulder as she passed by on her way to the kitchen, her daughter-in-law grasping her hand in a brief moment of comfort and solidarity.

CHAPTER FIFTEEN

It was a warm, humid morning and the walk to the bus stop in shirt sleeves had caused Ruairí to break out in a light sweat. School was becoming totally unbearable. He was falling behind in his schoolwork and Headmaster Finlay had written personally to Kathleen, his letter painting a very bleak picture. Ruairí only had to open his mouth and his mother would fly into a rage. She had changed so much since his father passed away. Some days she would be in bed when he came home, with Maeve staying behind to make the dinner.

When he was able to get away, he would cycle over to Oisín's house at Gurthalougha. From there, they would go to the treehouse or walk the fields. Ruairí and Aidan had become distant in recent months. He was unable to put his finger on the reason why, other than the simple fact that he didn't want to hang out with him. Oisín was different, more daring, and electrifying to be around. Out late one night, they found a tractor that had been left in a field by a farmer who had earlier been digging ditches.

"Whoa, hold your horses!" Oisín cried.

"What is it?"

"Old man Clarke has gone and left his tractor in the field!"

"Come on, Oisín, it's a great night, let's keep going," urged Ruairí.

"We'll just have a quick look; I always wanted to see the inside of a John Deere."

"What if he comes back for it?"

"Nah, he'll be in with the pigs, or watching TV."

The pair laid their bikes in the hedge and walked across the field to where the green and yellow tractor stood. Having finally got it started and, after a bit of gear crunching, Oisín proceeded to drive the machine with Ruairí standing behind him.

"This is fun!" laughed Ruairí over the noise of the engine as he looked around to see if anyone was coming.

"Here, you try," said Oisín, stopping abruptly.

Ruairí, having watched his friend, nervously rammed the tractor into gear and let the clutch out, causing the machine to jerk violently at first before making its way erratically through the meadow. With his speed increasing, and the engine's vibration coming through the steering wheel, he felt a sense of euphoria.

After a couple of laps, Oisín took charge again and began showing off as he tried to make the turn at the far end of the field. It all went into a state of slow motion, the fading light causing him to turn too late and lose control of the machine which ended up on its side in a drain.

Ruairí knew what was going to happen and held tightly on to a handle, spraining his elbow on a steel column. A little dazed, he looked to Oisín, who had cut his head in the accident. Opening the rear window, they clambered out and up the muddy bank.

"You're bleeding!" exclaimed Ruairí, as they climbed over the gate.

"I'm sure I'll live. That was deadly, wasn't it?"

"What am I going to tell my mam? My clothes are filthy!"

"I'm going to say I was taking a pee and I lost my footing."

"I hope nobody saw us, Oisín. I'm for it if my nana hears anything about this."

"Don't worry, no one's going to know, and Clarke will get one of his other tractors to pull it out. Let's make ourselves scarce!"

The pair collected their bikes and quickly headed to their respective homes before anyone came to investigate.

****

Ruairí put his bike in the barn and quietly crept upstairs, where he headed straight for the bathroom, but the door opened before he could slide the keeper across.

"And where have you been all night, Ruairí Delaney?" asked his mother, eyeing his clothes which were caked in clay.

"Nowhere."

"Where's nowhere? You said that you were going over to Aidan's tonight."

"I was, but I changed my mind," he lied.

Ruairí had told his mother that he was going to Aidan's house, but that was because she no longer approved of Oisín since he had been caught shoplifting in Birr. When she had first heard about it, Kathleen made it clear to Ruairí that he was to give Oisín a wide berth, both in school and outside of it.

“Where were you and who were you with?”

Ruairí chose not to answer, staring at the floor instead.

“I won’t ask you again, Ruairí, you didn’t get into that state riding your bike!” she shouted, becoming increasingly irritated.

“I was on my own, Mam, honest. I went for a run near Gurthalougha Forest and I tripped and fell. I’m sorry for getting my clothes dirty.”

“Get stripped off and into the bath. Do you not think I’ve enough to do without being at your beck and call? You need to take more responsibility for yourself, young man. In future, you don’t go anywhere unless I know exactly where you’ll be, is that understood?”

“Yes,” he replied sharply, before slamming the bathroom door closed.

Kathleen had no appetite to argue any further with Ruairí for the time being. She resolved to find out where he had been and why he had stopped running around with Aidan, who had always been such a positive influence on him. Kathleen could see that Ruairí was slowly beginning to slip through her fingers. Just like everything else in her life, their relationship was falling apart, and she was powerless to stop it.

****

“Well, if it isn’t Peggy McGrath! What’s enticed you back to Ballinderry again? I knew that sooner or later the glitz and glamour of Birr would lose its sparkle!”

"Check that tongue of yours, Maeve Delaney, or I'll line it with salt," chortled the old woman as she entered the shop. "And how are you?"

"I'm bearing up, as long as I keep myself busy. As the saying goes, an idle mind is a vessel for mischief!"

"Did you hear about old man Clarke's tractor being found on its side in a ditch?" she enquired, setting her handbag on the counter.

"Where was this, Peggy?"

"Near Gurthalougha. He had parked it there for the night and someone decided to fool around with it."

"They can leave nothing alone, Peggy. Sure, there were eggs taken from Ainsley's farm and smashed along the road; such a waste."

As she spoke, Ruairí burst through the door on his return from school.

"You weren't, by any chance, learning to drive a tractor, Master Ruairí?" asked the old woman jokingly.

Ruairí turned bright red, his cheeks burning with remorse.

"Peggy, will you act your age! Never mind her, pet, go you upstairs and your mam will make you some toast."

Ruairí went up to his room as the pair kept up their good-natured banter. Just then the doorbell rang and the Dutchwoman entered, shopping bag in hand. She greeted the women and headed to the rear of the store.

"Have you got to talk with her yet, Maeve?" whispered Peggy, not wanting to be overheard.

“I’ve no need to talk with her, I know who she is. Do you not recognise her?”

“No, for heaven’s sake, how would I know who the woman is? I haven’t spoken a word to her since she arrived!”

Maeve stopped to change the till roll before continuing the conversation.

“Do you remember the family that used to live near Luska? The father was a Dutchman.”

“Aye, I remember him alright, the boyo who put everything on the slate and upped and left, paying no one. That was an age past…. no, she can’t be…. is she a relative, Maeve?”

“We’ll find out in due course, but why else would she want to live in this quiet backwater? In all probability, she is his daughter and you can bet she’ll have left a trail of debt behind her, just like her father.”

“Oh, I don’t know, it was many moons ago and she would’ve only been a slip of a girl then. Give me my ten Woodbines and I’ll be gone,” requested Peggy, keen to be on her way.

Briege arrived at the counter where, without any chit-chat, Maeve rang each of her chosen items through slowly and methodically.

“That’ll be twenty-two punts, eighty-five…. in cash, please,” she said, with an icy stare.

Briege didn't grasp what Maeve was hinting at and paid in full for her provisions. Saying nothing, she packed her bag, put away her change and left the store.

****

Briege Geels felt as if the whole community was watching her every move - even though they weren't - as she rode back to Coolbawn. Everything seemed so alien to her. What had possessed her to come to Ireland in the first place; was it some romantic notion that it would make everything better again? It had been a lifetime since she had lived in Luska, far too long ago to even remember how many rooms were in her former home. She had no immediate family; her married stepsister lived on a farm in the Australian outback, and both of her parents had passed away within nine months of each other, eight years ago.

Briege's father had been a skilled cabinetmaker by trade. After opening a carpentry workshop in Birr, he often spent long periods away from home on construction jobs. When the firm suddenly collapsed, the family returned to Holland. Briege had once asked her mother why they had left Ireland. She told her there had been money problems and that had been the end of the matter.

The sun was quite high in the sky, a soft breeze partially lifting the hem of her summer dress. As she cycled along, sparrows flew out in front of her to intimidate her away from their nests. On a few occasions, she had been out for an early morning run on the bike and had spied Kathleen walking the roads, perhaps excising her inner turmoil as she herself had tried to do.

Briege knew that if she didn't have her trusty bike to get out and about on, and the Bechstein for periods of inclement weather, she would have given up by now. Not once though had she been able to pluck up enough courage to stop with the young widow just to talk with her for a moment or two, offer her a few words of consolation, or maybe even hold her hand. Briege had never been afforded that luxury when she lost her husband. She was left to grieve alone.

****

The sun rose at five thirty, the wild birds putting on a fanfare to greet its arrival. Two hours later, Ruairí rubbed the sleep from his eyes. He had tossed and turned all night, thinking about the farmer's tractor. The Gardaí had come to the school to give a lecture on road safety some days later but fortunately he had not referred to the incident. Out of the corner of his eye, he could see Oisín staring at him. Ruairí knew what they had done was wrong, but he had gotten a real buzz from it. The only downside had been the foul mood his mother was in for days afterwards.

Once dressed, he went to the kitchen and ate his breakfast whilst Kathleen drank her tea silently, looking at her son and wondering was his head in a similar mess to her own. She could not bring herself to ask him if he had been in the vicinity of Mr Clarke's farm, as they seemed to argue over the most trivial things nowadays. But his clothes had been covered in clay and oil and he didn't get that from just falling over.

As he fetched his coat from the hanger under the stairs, Ruairí's thoughts went to last night and *The Johan*. He had slipped out of the house unnoticed, and once by the Derg had hung back, under cover of the trees to avoid being seen. Through one of the boat's windows he could see Briege, who had her back to him, playing her beloved piano. The melodies had drifted from the boat unhindered, to be carried on the night air across the Derg as if on some unseen magic carpet. Works by Chopin, Debussy and Mozart, were just one more acute reminder of his father.

"Come on, Ruairí, hurry or you'll be late for the bus. Did you finish your homework?" asked Kathleen.

Ruairí came out of his reverie.

"Yes…. Can I have five punts?"

"For what? I've packed you a lunch."

"They're collecting for the nuns in Africa today."

"Are you sure? There was nothing in the parish bulletin, and I didn't hear Father Moloney announce it at Mass."

"Headmaster Finlay told us at assembly yesterday, but it doesn't matter," said Ruairí nonchalantly, putting his bag over his shoulder.

"Give me my purse…. they're always looking donations for something or other," said his mother, handing him the money. "Oh, and by the way, your nana will be picking you up from football practice."

"There is no football. Master Flynn cancelled, he has a meeting to go to," explained Ruairí.

“That school is getting worse. How are parents supposed to plan their day when they are not informed of any changes? Will you just go before you miss your bus!” said Kathleen tersely as she strode off to open the shop.

Arms crossed, she looked out of the window as Ruairí got on the bus; she had forgotten to give him a hug and a kiss, something she had always done since he was born. Tears welled up, blurring her vision, and she quickly wiped them away as she lifted the phone to make an appointment with Doctor Walsh.

CHAPTER SIXTEEN

Oisín made room for Ruairí as he boarded the bus.

"Where's your schoolbag, Oisín?" enquired Ruairí.

"In me mam's coal shed. I told you to leave yours at home!"

"Couldn't. Mam would've seen me, and she always knows when something's up."

"Never mind. We'll stash it someplace and pick it up on our way back. Where's the money?"

"In my pocket."

"How much?"

"Five punts."

"Is that all? You own a shop and you only bring five punts? Give it to me," demanded Oisín.

"Why? It's mine!"

"Alright. You can hang on to it for now," said Oisín as he dug his hands into his jacket pockets, satisfied he had money to fall back on if his scheme went wrong.

Ruairí was still unsure about the whole venture. He hated lying to his mother about the five punts but Oisín had insisted he brought money in case they needed it. They had agreed to bunk off school for the day, staying on the bus and travelling onwards to Birr instead. On arrival at the school gates everyone else got off, with Aidan giving them a dirty look as he walked by. Ruairí's eyes remained downcast as he surveyed an imaginary stain on the floor. The doors of the coach made a hissing sound as they closed, the driver scrutinising them in the rear-view mirror.

"I hope Finlay doesn't ring my mam," Ruairí fretted, now really having second thoughts about playing truant.

"He won't ring. I was missing for a week and no one came looking for me. Relax, I'll write you a letter saying that you were sick. It'll be cool, a day out on the town, and one of my pals might meet up with us."

"What if Aidan tells someone that we didn't get off the bus?"

"Ruairí, will you stop your whinging? I don't know why I decided to take you in the first place, you're beginning to get on my nerves!"

They sat in silence as the worn-out coach made its way to Birr. Ruairí had a knot in his stomach, which grew ever larger as their destination drew near. Something told him this day trip was a recipe for disaster. As he peered out of the window, his father's face scowled back at him with disgust written all over it. The bus came to a halt and the doors swung open.

"Are you two not supposed to be in school? Do your parents know about your little expedition?" asked the bus driver.

"Mind your own business!" sneered Oisín aggressively, propelling Ruairí down the steps and out on to the pavement.

There was no getting out of it now. He was somewhere that he shouldn't be and, all of a sudden, school seemed a better option if only he could catch the next bus back. Perhaps it wouldn't be so bad if he went in late, even though his mother would make mincemeat of him when he came home with a note from Headmaster Finlay.

They walked a few hundred yards to a supermarket, where Oisín hid Ruairí's schoolbag behind a large commercial bin.

"Where's the money your mam gave you?" he asked, putting his arm around Ruairí's shoulders in a friendly manner.

Trying to come up with something fast, Ruairí stuttered that he could have it later but, quickly pinning him up against a wall, Oisín issued an ultimatum.

"Hand it over, Ruairí, I won't ask you again."

Ruairí tried to pull away, but the blow stung his cheek as Oisín's fist struck him hard. He was rooted to the spot, scarcely believing what had just happened.

"Sorry, I didn't mean to be so rough," said Oisín, snatching the money from the breast pocket of Ruairí's shirt, "but you can be a right dose."

****

Having parked the car, Kathleen made her way down the street to the doctor's. On seeing Niamh O'Riordan walking towards her, she hurriedly crossed over. She wasn't ready for this; the memory of losing Patrick was too raw, and she had nothing to say to the woman. When Niamh began to call out her name, she put her head down and quickened her pace into the surgery where the doctor was awaiting her arrival.

"Thank you for seeing me, Doctor Walsh," she panted, trying to catch her breath.

"Not at all, Kathleen. Take a seat, you look like you need it. What can I do for you?"

"I'm feeling constantly exhausted, Doctor, but I can't sleep, and I'm very irritable. The slightest thing sets me off. Poor Ruairí's getting the brunt of it."

"This must be a testing time for all of you, Kathleen. Let's take your blood pressure and see how we can help," said the doctor as he put in place the monitoring equipment. "It appears to be a little low, and you look as if you've lost weight too. Are you eating regularly?"

"Yes, Ruairí needs to have a routine so, yes, I am eating regularly."

"When we're finished here, I want you to go to the nurse and have a few blood samples taken. I'm going to prescribe a course of iron tablets for you to take in the meantime and, when the results come back, I'll have a better idea of any other medication you may need."

"If it wasn't for my son …."

Kathleen broke down, the doctor handing her a box of tissues.

"I'm sorry, Doctor, but I'm finding it so hard to cope. The shop, everyday life, there's no end to it, and on top of everything else I feel as if I'm losing Ruairí. We don't share the close bond that he and his father had."

"Kathleen, children are, if nothing else, resilient. They feed off positive energy, so you must be strong for him. You're the adult; try to put yourself in his young shoes. You both need to give it time."

"Thanks again, Doctor, talking to you has really helped," she said as she stood up to leave.

"One more thing, Kathleen, have you considered the possibility that you may be pregnant? Have your cycles been regular?"

Stunned, Kathleen sank into the chair again as it all began to make sense. For many years, she had simply accepted the prospect that she would never have any more children. She had not had the opportunity to stop and think until now, but the signs were all there. Kathleen concluded that it must have happened during their break in Cork.

"I don't know whether I'm coming or going, Doctor, but there is a chance, now that you mention it. It's been a while since my last period. I had put it down to stress. Oh my God, this is all I need on top of everything else! I can't afford to lose another child; it's a gift from Patrick growing inside me."

"Now, don't be fretting, Kathleen, but I need you to provide the nurse with a urine sample and we'll take it from there. You must endeavour to get as much rest as you can; with your history of miscarriages, this is a critical time for you," said Doctor Walsh as he walked her to the door.

****

"Hi, Jono, how's things?" asked Oisín as a scruffy looking teenager sauntered up to them.

"Ah, you know, the usual crap. Is this the little fella you were telling me about?" he replied, giving Ruairí the once-over.

"Yep, keen as mustard. Looks the part too!"

Ruairí was feeling ill at ease. He didn't like the look of this person and, by the sound of it, the meeting had been prearranged.

"Come on, let's go for a mooch around town and see what's on offer."

Ruairí tugged at Oisín's sleeve, muttering that he needed to speak with him.

"What is it?" Oisín snapped.

"I want to go home," whispered Ruairí, his voice trembling.

"You listen to me, pal, we've a job lined up and we need your help to carry it off. You're staying until it's done," he whispered menacingly, tapping him on the cheek before falling in with Jono.

Ruairí reluctantly followed behind. He felt sick, and was more than perturbed about what they had in mind for him.

****

They arrived at a convenience store, where they gazed through the window while checking out the street for anyone who might interfere with their plans.

"Now, there's only two women in today so it'll be grand as long as your little helper doesn't screw it up," hissed Jono.

"He won't," Oisín immediately replied, elbowing Ruairí in the side.

"Fair enough, mate. Now then, Ruairí, I want you to head to the alcohol aisle and smash three or four bottles as a distraction. Meanwhile, Oisín and me will be busy at the till. Understood?"

Ruairí froze. They were going to rob the store and he was to act as a decoy!

"No, I won't do it, it's wrong; I'm leaving!"

Jono had him by the throat before he could flee, nearly throttling him.

"Now, look here, you little toerag, I've been working on this for weeks. If you don't go through with it you'll be crawling home, minus that cute smile! Now do we understand each other?"

Locked in fear, Ruairí made no reply.

Jono repeated the order, while gripping Ruairí ever tighter.

"We're all partners in this, bud, and your job is smashing bottles. Comprende?"

Ruairí nodded. On top of everything else, Jono's putrid breath was vile, making him want to throw up. Having been released from his grip, Ruairí waited on the signal to go into the store.

"When we get in, turn left and make for the off-licence section," ordered Jono. "I want to hear you making a right racket but don't worry, you're underage so they can't do anything on you."

As in the shop at home in Ballinderry, a bell sounded when the threesome entered. Two female cashiers stood behind the counter, engaged in small talk whilst eyeing them with suspicion. How Ruairí longed to walk straight up to them and tell them what was about to happen, but Oisín and Jono were stuck to him like glue. As they forced him to make his way towards the alcohol section, he stopped dead in his tracks until one of the shop assistants asked Oisín if she could help him. The bottles seemed to fall in slow motion as Ruairí swiped them off the shelves, the sound of breaking glass bringing the other member of staff running in his direction.

Jono hit the button on the cash register, the drawer popping open with a muffled chime. The money was pocketed in seconds and they were out the door, leaving Ruairí behind, cornered by one of the women as the other went to call the Gardaí. Shortly thereafter, two burly guards arrived and detained him, while Jono and Oisín were picked up a few streets away and taken to Birr Garda Station to be processed. With some hesitancy, Ruairí eventually gave his name and address.

****

Kathleen had arrived back from the health centre. Having set her handbag down on the kitchen table, she was filling the kettle when the phone rang. It was a Garda officer, informing her that Ruairí was in custody following the foiled robbery.

"But my son's in school, there must be some mistake!" said Kathleen with incredulity.

"I know this will come as a bit of a shock to you, madam, but the lad provided us with this number and gave his name as Ruairí Delaney."

Feeling faint, Kathleen pulled over a chair.

"What happens now? Will he be charged?"

"The store has agreed not to press charges, Mrs Delaney. According to an eyewitness on the street, your son was forced to take part in the crime, and we are letting him off with a caution. Believe me, he has had a close shave with these characters. I've asked two of my colleagues to bring Ruairí home when the paperwork's finished, so he'll be back with you soon."

Kathleen thanked the man and placed the phone back on the receiver. It was no mistake, Ruairí had been involved in an attempted robbery and Oisín Halloran was behind it. How many times had she cautioned him to stay away from that boy? It would be all over the village, not that she cared anymore. The hurt Kathleen felt could not get any worse. Let the moaning minnies say what they wanted, her son was all she had left and everyone else could go to hell.

CHAPTER SEVENTEEN

"What was that all about?" asked Maeve, who'd been trying to look busy when she came into the room but had been eavesdropping on the conversation.

Gathering her thoughts, Kathleen didn't reply at first. Ruairí, her little boy, being held in a Garda station! She couldn't get her head around it.

"That was the guards. They've taken Ruairí into custody, for attempted robbery."

"Away with you! Our Ruairí, a robbery? That can't be right, Kathleen, sure he's at school, isn't he?"

"Not a bit of it, Maeve, he was lifted at a convenience store in Birr. My son, of all people! Oisín Halloran and some other reprobate were also taken into custody. I told him not to be running around with that rapscallion but not a bit of notice did he take of me! They'll be bringing him home before long and, let me tell you, he'd better have one heck of a reason as to why he's been caught up in all of this!"

Kathleen went to the bathroom, locking the door behind her, and opened the pregnancy test kit she had bought from the chemist. Minutes seemed like hours before the device read positive. The procedure was then repeated with a second kit, which provided an identical result.

According to her calculations, Kathleen was nearly three months gone. Packing everything away, she flushed the toilet and went into the kitchen, her thoughts returning to her son who was, at this very moment, in the back of a Garda car.

"They're here!" Maeve shouted up to Kathleen, as the vehicle drove to the back of the property.

"Mrs Delaney, my name is Garda Ciara Brennan," said a young woman, helping Ruairí from the car.

Ruairí did not utter a word, or even dare to catch his mother's eye, as they all went upstairs.

"Go straight to your room and I'll deal with you later," said Kathleen in a gruff voice.

Ruairí did as he was told, closing the door softly behind him.

"What on earth's been going on?" asked Kathleen once they were seated.

"Your son simply got mixed up with a pair of real troublemakers, Mrs Delaney. I wouldn't be too hard on him. From the statements given, it appears that Ruairí was assaulted, and coerced into assisting the other two individuals to commit a robbery. One of them is known to us, a would-be drug dealer in the making."

"Is that Oisín Halloran?"

"No, another person, but that's all I'm prepared to say at this point."

"Ruairí would never have gone to Birr, nor taken part in any robbery, had it not been for that boy!"

"Maybe so, but Halloran alleges that your son went of his own free will, knowing full well what was to take place and the part he would play."

"What did Ruairí have to say for himself? Things have not been easy for him after losing his father recently."

"He said very little while he was in custody. One of our guys knew the circumstances of your husband's passing and, together with the fact that Ruairí has never been involved in any criminality before, we decided not to take the matter any further. It's the old adage, Mrs Delaney, he was just in the wrong place at the wrong time. Well, I'd best be going."

Kathleen walked Garda Brennan to her car. Her head felt ready to explode, such was the migraine she had. She didn't know whether to be furious with her son for disobeying her or pity him for what he had gone through. She decided to go and speak with him. On reaching the top of the stairs, she heard Maeve giving Ruairí the third degree.

"Are you going to answer me, Ruairí Delaney? You're a disgrace, that's what you are, and your poor father barely in his grave! How are we to hold our heads high in the village now….?"

"That's enough, Maeve, I'd like to speak with Ruairí alone, please," said Kathleen, unable to face another confrontation.

"I was…."

"Not now, Maeve!"

Her mother-in-law turned on her heel and went back to the shop, feeling like a schoolgirl who had just been chided by the headmistress.

"Why, Ruairí, just tell me why…. why did you not just go to school?" asked his mother, now with a steely resolve.

Ruairí hung his head in shame.

"Oisín made me do it!"

"You had a choice to get off the bus; why did you decide it was better to go to Birr with him?"

"I just told you, he made me do it!"

"I don't believe you now that you've taken up telling tall tales…. we have a little liar in our midst, feeding us with excuses."

"I'm not a liar, I'm telling you the truth, Mam, honest!"

"Like you did when you were supposed to be with Aidan Donnelly but you were actually spending your evenings with Oisín Halloran? That was all lies, was it not? Perhaps you pair were responsible for the tractor that mysteriously fell over into a ditch? I wouldn't put it past either of you."

"Mam, I'm telling you the truth. Oisín made me do everything today, it was all planned. I'm really sorry, you've got to believe me!"

"Not as sorry as I am, I can't rely on a single word you say anymore. And another thing, don't ever go near that Dutchwoman or her boat again, do you hear me? Your father and I have always told you to keep away from strangers. Now, go to your room until I say you can come out; I can't bear to look at you!"

Ruairí bolted back off to his bedroom, slamming the door behind him.

Kathleen had listened intently as Maeve filled her in on the Dutchman Anders de Wit, who had formerly lived in the area. De Wit had earned a reputation for buying materials from suppliers and never settling his accounts, as well as for failing to carry out jobs that his customers had paid up front for. Maeve wasn't a hundred per cent sure if Briege Geels was related, but she was a stranger to the area and that was reason enough for Ruairí not to be anywhere near her barge, or whatever it was she called it.

More than anything however, it was Oisín and his current behaviour that alarmed Kathleen. The other day, she had bumped into an old friend who had given her an account of the full extent of the Halloran family's problems. She felt nothing but compassion towards Oisín. No child should have been exposed to the brutality he had experienced, and perhaps today's incident was his way of striking back, a cry for help. And yet, selfish as her thoughts were, protecting Ruairí had to be her first and only concern right now.

****

Ruairí lay on the bed, his eyes burning as tears streamed down his face. His mother's words had cut through him like a knife. He knew he'd done wrong but how could she be so unkind to him? If only his father hadn't left - *died* - he found it hard to say that word. It was used to describe when a person was never coming back, and he was not yet ready to accept that fact. Ruairí would wake each morning, looking at the doorway of his room, yearning for Patrick to come walking through, as tall as a tree. He was sorry, sorry for everything, but he was not a liar; a liar was a person who made things up just to hurt others. He would never do that.

Mam thinks she's the only one who's hurting. She shuts herself away in the bedroom, never asking how I'm doing. I wish I was gone from here, there's nothing to smile or laugh about anymore. Dad took all that with him, said Ruairí to himself, wiping his nose on the sleeve of his shirt. Getting up, he quietly put on his coat and crept out onto the landing. His mother was lying down on the sofa. He tip-toed downstairs where Maeve was at the counter reading a paper, while two customers were picking out their groceries. It was now or never.

Having managed to steal away, Ruairí went straight to the barn. Lifting the Raleigh racing bike over the gate, he steered it out onto the road and set off in the direction of Gurthalougha Forest. Now and again, tears would form, dispersed by the wind rushing by him. He felt so alone. Even Nana was against him. She didn't love him anymore, too interested in what everybody would say. Dad wouldn't have stood for it, but there again he would never have let things become the way they were now.

****

Kathleen looked at the clock on the wall. She had been asleep for over an hour. *Ruairí will be starving*, she thought as she went to his room to fetch him. His bedroom was empty and, having searched the rest of the house, she went downstairs where Maeve was ringing through a customer's order.

"Maeve, have you seen Ruairí? I can't find him anywhere!"

Given their earlier exchange, Maeve was in two minds whether to reply or not, though now was not the time to continue the argument. She knew she had been wrong in reprimanding her grandson and wanted to make amends.

"The last I saw of him, he was in his room," she said as the customer left the shop.

"He must've took to his heels when I dozed off.... I ought to apologise for speaking to you in such a fashion, Maeve, it was uncalled for."

"I'm the one who should be apologising. I had no right to talk to the lad the way I did."

"I'm pregnant, Maeve!" Kathleen suddenly exclaimed.

"To tell you the truth, I've had my suspicions for a while now, pet, but I kept my big nose out of it. Goodness knows there's enough going on without me causing more strife."

The two women crossed the room and held one another, the jagged barrier between them dissolving into a united bond.

"I don't want to phone the guards again, Maeve, they're not long away."

"He'll be back, Kathleen, sure he's not eaten for most of the day. Most likely he's cheesed off with everyone for having a go at him and just needs a little space."

The two women went out to the barn and spied the road racer missing.

"He'll be burning off some of that Delaney rage, I'm sure. His father was the…."

Maeve stopped herself from finishing the sentence.

"You're right, Maeve, Patrick could holler with the best of them when he wanted to. I'll give Ruairí a while and then I'll go and look for him," said Kathleen as she turned to go back indoors.

****

Ruairí's temper had not waned. Mam and Nana had always said everyone needed a second chance in life but today proved that they were hypocrites. The next thing, he would be paraded in front of Father Moloney for a 'super confession'. He had been told that you could get twenty Hail Marys and ten Our Fathers if the priest deemed your sins to be extremely grave. Ruairí hadn't noticed his speed increasing, just as a sharp bend neared before Coolbawn Quay. Briege Geels idly rounded the corner on her bike and Ruairí began to panic, not wanting to collide with the woman. The Raleigh wobbled, giving way below him and, falling from the bike, he slid along the tarmac, the crash helmet taking most of the blows before he ended up in a ditch.

"You poor thing! Are you alright?" asked the woman as she ran over to him, her heavy accent making the word *alright* sound slurred.

"I'm fine, I'm fine," said Ruairí, in a hurry to lift the bike and be on his way.

"But you're not fine, your trouser leg is torn, and your knee is cut. It needs attention."

"I'm sorry for nearly running you down but I'll be okay, I don't live too far from here."

"I know who you are, you're the boy from the store. Your mother would have something to say if I let you leave in that condition! The wound has got to be sterilised, and a dressing applied."

Ruairí looked down at his leg. More trouble, he thought, they had been his best school trousers and now they were ruined. Everything he did seemed to go wrong. The morning spent in a Garda station, and now this. Why did he leave the house when he had been told to stay in his room?

He tried to ease past the woman and make his escape, but she was having none of it.

"Come with me, my barge is much closer than your house. I have a first aid kit there and I will fix you up as good as new."

Rather than cause another scene, Ruairí got on his bike and they headed to the little harbour at Coolbawn, the woman making no attempt to engage him in conversation as they made their way down the deserted road. Slightly apprehensive, he was nevertheless curious as to what the boat looked like inside.

CHAPTER EIGHTEEN

Having propped their bikes up against a drystone wall, Briege led the way on board the old converted freighter. It was a strange sensation being on something so large as it swayed on the water.

"Are you going to stand there all day looking around, or will we get you patched up? I'm sure your poor mother is wondering where you are. Does she know you're out?"

Ruairí shyly shook his head. As he walked in, he was astounded by the sheer scale of the dwelling, which was as big as a house. The walls were lined with the finest pine, as was the floor, which had been sealed with a delicate coating of varnish. A calming scent, like strawberries, heather and lavender all rolled into one, pervaded the air.

"Well, we'd best get started. Please, sit down so I can roll up that trouser leg and see how much of you there is left!" she joked, trying to put him at ease whilst opening the first aid box. "By the way, I am Mr Geels, what's your name?"

"It's Ruairí, Ruairí Delaney." he replied before taking a seat on an old couch.

Looking around the woman's home, Ruairí found it snug and inviting. For some reason, he felt at peace here. It had a peculiar silence and, if you listened closely enough, you could hear the water gently tickling the belly of the hull. His train of vision stopped abruptly, a little way down the boat. An upright black piano stood majestically against the wall, its stool resting on an old, red Persian-style rug. Ruairí was just about able to make out the manufacturer's name which was in an elaborate script: *Bechstein*. It sounded German.

His attention was brought into sharp focus as to why he was here, and he winced, stifling a cry as the cotton bud full of antiseptic touched his knee, sending out intense pain in response.

"You must be brave, little man. This needs to be done, otherwise infection comes. The bike won't be much good to you with only one leg," she chuckled, as her patient tried to hold back a smile. "Why were you travelling so fast on such a narrow road? You could have caused much hurt to someone, don't you agree? I am not like a cat, I have only one life!"

Ruairí was mesmerised by this lady's gentle demeanour. She did not shout at him or judge him. She just let him be.

"I wish I had had a son like you. You will enchant many young ladies when you are older, for sure," said Briege, using tweezers to extract the last of the gravel from the cut.

She covered the laceration with a large plaster and rolled the leg of Ruairí's trousers back down again.

"Now, I'll make us some tea, Ruairí," Briege said, walking over and placing the kettle on the stove.

When she turned around, she half expected to see the door ajar and the boy gone but she was pleased to find he had not left. She was intrigued that Ruairí had agreed to come to her home in the first place. Briege glanced over at him as she filled the teapot with boiling water and left it to draw on a low heat. Though she had never had children of her own, she was still able to see right through him. Briege could sense every nerve of his being crying out to be mended, but by whom?

****

Ruairí rested quietly on *The Johan* for nearly an hour. Lying stretched out on the sofa, at ease with this woman, he merely nodded when asked if he would like more tea. She had put two sugars in his first cup, which made him feel better, and he had already enjoyed two of her homemade cinnamon pastries. Once she had placed the cups and plates in the sink, Briege sat down at her piano and softly played, allowing Ruairí some time to himself. When she went to check on him, he was gone.

****

Ruairí's leg was now throbbing as he climbed the short ascent, passing the road to Gurthalougha Forest. He hoped that the lady had not been offended by his abrupt departure; she had been so kind to him. In his head, he went over and over those words, those very special words she had said, that she wished she had had a son like him. At least someone cared. She was a stranger but, somehow, he felt that he already knew her.

As he neared the shop, the school bus was pulling away from its stop, providing a timely reminder of the day he had just had. Why hadn't he got off the bus as he always did? He was finished with Oisín. He was supposed to be a friend, but real friends didn't hit you and take all your money before forcing you to help rob from someone who had done nothing to deserve it.

His thoughts went to Aidan and his eyes welled with tears. He missed him so much. How could he make things right with his real friend? The nights out lamping, hours spent in the treehouse talking nonsense. And then there was Liam, and Donal too. They could all be heading to the forest around now, where they would horse around before cooling off in the waters of the Derg.

Ruairí cycled on and around to the barn, heaving the bike over the fence. He tried to figure out what to say. Once again, there would be an argument as he wasn't supposed to be anywhere near the Dutchwoman's boat. He lingered outside for a while before heading in to face the music.

****

"What have you gone and done now?" asked Kathleen as she viewed her son's torn trousers.

"I had an accident, that's all."

"Look at the state of you! Why didn't you change before you went out? Money doesn't grow on trees, you know. Let me see your leg."

"It's fine. I'll go and put my tracksuit bottoms on."

"Take off those pants, I'm sure that cut will need dressing."

Ruairí looked at his mother and then looked away, afraid to undress as she would see the fresh plaster. After a moment's hesitation, he ran to his room and closed the door, with Kathleen following in hot pursuit. She found him sitting on the bed and, on checking his leg, it was evident that someone had already attended to the cut.

"Who did this, Ruairí?"

He remained uncommunicative. Whatever he said, he was in trouble. How he wished he was back on the barge, with all the sweet smells and kindness that a real home should have.

"I won't ask you again, young man, tell me who did this!" shouted Kathleen, startling her son; she knew that if any of the neighbours had seen to him, they would have phoned to let her know. It was as clear as day to Kathleen where Ruairí had been.

"You're just as stubborn as your father, Ruairí Delaney! From now on, there'll be no more football, you'll come straight back here and do your homework. I've had the school on and your grades are atrocious! How do you propose to get into St. Joseph's? And another thing, that bike is not to leave the yard. There'll be no more secret jaunts down to Coolbawn Quay for you!"

Ruairí shook his head in defeat; there was no point in arguing. *Even Mam doesn't like Dad anymore. I wish I was a million miles from here. All everyone does is shout and blame me when there's trouble. No one asks what's going on in my life. I have things that need fixing, just like the grown-ups, but no one wants to listen. I might have bled to death if the Dutchwoman hadn't patched me up,* he exaggerated to himself, *yet I'm not allowed to go near her, or breathe her name.*

Dinner was burgers, chips and baked beans, with a large slice of resentment separating mother and son at the table that night. Maeve had bingo with her friends, so she went home to change. Later, as Kathleen started the ironing, her mood had not lifted. She was determined to find out who had ministered to her son and looked in on him every now and then in case he decided to try and sneak out again. Grounding Ruairí would cause even more tension, but he needed to learn that actions had consequences. His father was no longer there to keep him in check; she would have to be both mother and father to her son from now on.

****

A week had passed, and nothing seemed to have changed much in the Delaney household. Ruairí's frame of mind had not improved and he was keeping more and more to himself. Doctor Walsh's prescription of iron supplements seemed to be working though, and Kathleen was faring better.

"Come in, Kathleen, take a seat. How are you?"

"I'm feeling good, Doctor, thank you. I couldn't wait for the results and I bought a couple of home test kits myself."

"And I'm sure they were in keeping with our findings, weren't they?"

Even though she knew she was expecting, hearing confirmation from the doctor unsettled her. She was apprehensive about coping with her pregnancy alone.

"I'm both amazed and ecstatic, but it's very early days so I won't get my hopes up, given my track record. Maeve's aware of my condition and I thought it best not to tell Ruairí, for the moment at least."

“That may be a wise decision, under the circumstances. I will arrange for you to have a hospital scan in a few weeks’, so we can keep an eye on things but, if you have any concerns in the interim, contact the surgery right away. Remember, I’m always on the end of a phone, Kathleen. Now, is there anything else you need?”

“No, thanks, Doctor. If I can just get through the next few months, I’ll be in with a chance this time.”

****

It was a misty morning as the bus drew up to its stop. Ruairí’s breath stuck in his throat; sitting by the window was Oisín. He hadn’t anticipated seeing him again so soon. Maeve had read in the Gazette that Oisín had been placed in a young offenders’ centre while his case for robbing the supermarket was being processed through the courts. Ruairí got on, head bowed low, and chose a seat near the front, hoping against hope that Oisín would leave him alone. His fears were realised however when his now ex-friend strolled up the aisle and sat down beside him as the bus trundled on to the next halt.

“Are you avoiding me, Delaney? Am I nothing but a waster now?”

“I’m not allowed to be with you,” Ruairí replied in a timorous voice.

“Says who? Do you have any money?”

“Says my mam, and I only have enough for the tuck shop.”

“Give it to me!”

“It’s mine, Oisín, why are you being like this?”

"Just hand it over and quit your whining," he said, slapping him on the back of the head.

Ruairí obeyed the order and gave Oisín the punt that his nana had left out on the table for him that morning. The bus reached its next stop and Aidan, along with a gaggle of chattering schoolgirls, got on.

"Open your mouth about this and I'll shut it for you," threatened Oisín before transferring to another seat.

Ruairí was shaking. He felt so helpless but who could he tell? His mother wouldn't believe him. He had thought that Oisín would have to remain in the young offenders' centre at least until his trial, Nana had assured him of that. When they got to school, he kept to himself for the rest of the day. This wasn't hard to do as, by now, everyone had got the message. Yet he wanted more than ever to be friends with Aidan again.

****

Some days later, with Kathleen having relaxed his curfew, Ruairí took the bike out for a run. He was torn. Oisín was still bullying him and taking his pocket money, threatening to bring Jono with him to rob the store if he didn't do as he was told. Ruairí was almost sick each time Oisín came near him. More than ever, he felt desolate and bereft without his father.

He rode down to Coolbawn Quay, the water, as smooth as glass, allowing a gentle breeze to drift inland. Nearby, willows floated back and forth in a lazy waltz, the weight of the birds' nests acting like a pendulum. The soft sound of a piano filled the air as a light mist began to roll inland. Ruairí was bewitched; he could literally feel the notes caress his ears.

He was not quite ready to approach the woman yet. Whilst she had shown him a great act of kindness by tending to his leg, he was uncertain how she would react to him turning up unannounced. Briege's tempo remained steady throughout, the soulful melodies drawing him ever closer.

Ruairí stepped onboard *The Johan* and gently tapped on the door.

"Come in, please, you are most welcome!" said Briege with an engaging smile. "Won't you sit down?"

Ruairí took a seat, shedding his coat as Briege began to play once more. He said little, savouring the music as each note was teased from the worn ebony and ivory keys. Briege did not mind his silence. She made no demands on him, pleased only that he had thought enough of her to return. Not wanting to outstay his welcome, Ruairí remained there for half an hour before politely making his excuses to leave. Having put his coat back on - zipped up to the neck - he fetched his bike from behind a hedge and, with great reluctance, headed home.

CHAPTER NINETEEN

"Hello, Kathleen," said Maeve chirpily as she arrived to start her shift.

"And what has you in such high spirits today, Maeve?" asked Kathleen.

"Sure, look around you! It's only June and the sun is splitting the trees; what more could you ask for? How are you keeping? No more morning sickness?"

"Thank God that's away and this old body's eventually coming to terms with motherhood again. I'm a bit concerned for Ruairí though, he's begun wetting the bed."

Maeve stopped in mid-flight and looked at Kathleen.

"How long has this been going on?"

"Two weeks now, and I don't know what the cause is. It would have been understandable when…."

There was a slight pause, an awkwardness in finding the right words.

"…. when Patrick passed away. It's not like him. I know he's a handful at present, but there's something not right with him."

"It's all down to that brigand O'Riordan! He hasn't the foggiest notion of the harm he has caused. That child is traumatised for life because Patrick could never say no to a friend. Those O'Riordans are not to set foot over this threshold ever again, Kathleen, do you hear me?"

"Now, now, Maeve, don't be getting yourself worked up. It's Ruairí we have to concentrate on," said Kathleen, hoping to calm the old woman.

"You're right, Kathleen, Ruairí needs our support to see him through this. Have you spoken with Dr Walsh yet?"

"He says that, given everything that Ruairí has been through recently, it will just take time for him to readjust."

"Do you think a few sessions with a grief counsellor would help?" asked Maeve.

"Frankly, Maeve, I don't know what will help anymore," Kathleen replied.

****

Ruairí was walking down the corridor, past the locker room, when he was grabbed by the scruff of his neck and dragged inside.

"I called over to you twice today and you just ignored me," said Oisín, with a twisted smile on his face.

Ruairí tried to break free but was being held tight against the wall.

"I'm in enough trouble at home, Oisín, please, don't make things any worse than they already are," he pleaded.

"But you haven't even heard about Jono's latest project yet! That's not the way friends behave is it, or…. perhaps you're not my friend?"

"I am, really I am, but Mam's been having a tough time and I don't want to cause her any more aggravation. Why can't you just leave me be?"

"You do one more little job for me and Jono, and I won't bother you again."

"No, I got into enough…."

Oisín slapped Ruairí across the face before he could complete the sentence.

"This is not a request, Delaney," he continued in a hushed voice, "you're coming with me to Birr tomorrow morning, got that? Jono will be waiting for us. The bread man will be delivering to another shop in Birr and he's always got a wad of cash in that big leather bag of his. This job is a piece of cake! Get it? What's wrong, lost your sense of humour?"

Ruairí's stomach was churning. He hoped and prayed that someone would walk in and disturb them, allowing him to get away.

"I won't do it! I won't be getting lifted by the guards again, not for you or anybody else, so…."

His voice tailed off as Halloran struck him in the ribs, partially winding him.

"If you know what's good for you, you'll be on the bus tomorrow morning, or else!"

With that last threat, he left Ruairí crumpled up on the floor. The bell sounded for afternoon break. Ruairí sat up against the wall, holding his side and wiping tears on the sleeve of his jumper. How was he going to get out of this mess? If he took a day off school, the headmaster would ring his mam immediately. His gut instinct told him that by tomorrow they would all be back in Emmet Square, Oisín, Jono and himself, the hare-brained scheme having failed once more. This time, the guards would not be so lenient with him. He would be in real bother and there was a danger that Social Services would be called in, as had happened with the Halloran family.

"Ruairí, what on earth are you doing in here, sitting in the dark?" asked Mrs O'Reilly, who taught the Junior Infants class. "Get yourself out into the fresh air; it might keep you awake for Master Rankin!"

Ruairí hurried off and went to the toilet instead, fearful of running into Oisín again.

****

Feeling much better, Kathleen had made an extra effort with dinner and had prepared lasagne, her son's favourite. She was concerned when he barely touched it, which was unlike him. Ruairí had become withdrawn following his father's death but tonight he barely said two words during their meal. His mother found it increasingly difficult to speak with him when he didn't want to engage in conversation. Yet she knew something was really troubling him. Standing in the kitchen, she took a long look at the most precious thing she had, next to the baby she hoped to deliver. Ruairí sat motionless, staring at the wall and it was then that she noticed the weight loss.

Around eight o'clock, Kathleen got a bath ready, adding her best aromatherapy oils. From this day forward, she promised herself that she would do everything in her power to get back the child she had once held in her arms. She went to fetch some fresh towels from the hot press and, upon her return, she found Ruairí already undressing. Kathleen could not help but see the bruising on her son's ribs.

Taking a deep breath, she closed the door quietly behind her and sank to the floor on the other side. Instinct told her that Oisín Halloran was behind this. Should she begin to quiz Ruairí tonight or wait until he had had a good sleep? Her feelings ran from sorrow to anger that anyone could have done this to her son. Kathleen decided to play it by ear in the morning.

****

Ruairí eased himself into the tub, avoiding the bruised area which was still tender. He was relieved that his mother hadn't noticed as that would have led to another row. Maybe he should stand his ground with Oisín tomorrow and punch him square on the nose, like in the old Laurel and Hardy films he and his dad used to watch together. But that was in the movies; in reality, he was no match for Oisín.

Towelling himself dry, he got into fresh pyjamas and went to his room where he knelt on the ottoman by the window. There was a full moon, casting an eerie blanket of grey over the fields. Seeking a mate, a lone fox called out and, some way off, a barn owl answered back, perhaps laying down a challenge. Ruairí glanced over at the empty box under his bed, where his cycling magazines had been. He was still unable to figure out why he had acted in such an appalling manner. Even so, cycling was of little interest to him now that he no longer had his father to share it with. He heard his mother putting the ironing board away and scrambled into bed, pulling the blankets tightly around his neck, pretending to be asleep.

Kathleen came into the room and sat on the edge of the bed. The moon now shed its light on the old tallboy, picking out stickers that Ruairí had placed there when he was about five. Kathleen ran her hand through his hair; she was beginning to lose Ruairí and she didn't know how to stop it. She kissed his brow and made a silent prayer, asking God to watch over and protect both her son and the child she was carrying.

****

Briege, dressed in a thick, woollen cardigan and black leggings, brought a camping seat on deck. There was not a breeze to be found and the water glistened like fine crystal. The stillness was broken only by trout rising to catch flies near the surface. It was on nights like this her loneliness became apparent; she would have traded this idyllic quietness for the noisy city life of Rotterdam just to have her husband by her side. She had toyed with the idea of getting a dog for companionship but felt it was too soon to bring a living creature into her life.

Briege was undecided as to how much longer she would remain at Coolbawn. She had few callers, which suited her fine at the moment but, someday, she would have to let go and get on with her life, though what form that would take she could not envision. Her thoughts drifted to the Delaney child and his mother. She hadn't seen him much recently and, when he did call round, he said little, preferring to sit quietly and look out onto the waters, lost in his thoughts. Such heartache had been visited upon the young family. Kathleen seemed a strong woman, but would she be strong enough to get her and the boy through this difficult time?

In the distance, she glimpsed the faint light of a fishing boat as it made its way to the shore a little further up the lough, the rhythmic beat of its engine growing ever louder. With a chill setting in, Briege folded the camp chair and made her way below deck, locking the door for the night and placing another log on the fire. Opening some sheet music, she sat down and began to play a Schumann *Romance*. She was captivated by the haunting melody and had once read that it was the last piece of music that his wife, Clara, had heard before her death. It had been much-loved by Johan, especially on those languid Sunday mornings alone together, with the canal veiled in mist.

****

"Did you sleep well, darling?" Kathleen enquired from her position at the stove as Ruairí came in for breakfast.

He merely grunted in reply, switching on the radio to drown out any more questions. He could hardly find the energy to get out of bed this morning. His nightmares had returned, only this time more vividly. The dragons were thrashing around the living room now, and demons were throwing records everywhere. He chased them, and they flew out of the windows, heading back to Gurthalougha. Following behind, he caught sight of his father running towards him, but the beasts were dragging him back into the darkness. Ruairí fought them with his wooden sword, until the dream left him for a fitful sleep.

The eggs hissed and spat at Kathleen as she flicked them with hot oil; her son liked them runny. The bruising on Ruairí's body weighed heavily on her mind. She was resolved to try and speak with him. Perhaps she would even call with Headmaster Finlay and ask him to keep a closer eye on Ruairí.

"Come on, sleepyhead, breakfast is ready!"

He slumped down on his chair at the table. Bacon, eggs, potato bread and a dollop of red sauce were laid out on the plate in front of him, along with a steaming mug of tea. He looked up at his mother as she set out her own breakfast. If he began to tell her what Oisín Halloran was planning for the day, she would just go off on one of her rants. She was sure to blame him and say that if he didn't talk to Oisín then he wouldn't get himself into such predicaments.

I wish things could go back to the way they were before Dad.... why didn't he just let the O'Riordans look after their own cattle?.... Everything I do nowadays is wrong. I'm just a liar to Mam and even Nana called me a disgrace! She's more interested in what people are saying about us than how I feel....

Ruairí's thoughts trailed off as he popped the yoke of the egg into his mouth. That gave him some comfort, cutting the yoke from the white and allowing the warm fluid to burst in his mouth.

Kathleen sat down. Looking up at the clock, she saw it was just after half past eight. She desperately wanted to broach the subject of her son's injuries. The following week they would be off for the summer break, but she decided to push the matter.

"How are things at school, Ruairí? Mr Finlay says you have done well in all your tests."

"I know, he told me," was the brusque reply.

"Why didn't you say? You would let me know if there was something wrong, wouldn't you?"

"I forgot."

"I just want to know you're safe, that's all."

"You don't need to keep checking up on me, Mam! I have to go or I'll be late for school."

Ruairí rose from his chair, put on his coat and slung his schoolbag over one shoulder.

"Have you got everything?" asked Kathleen.

"Yes. Bye," he replied as he left the house.

Kathleen was just about to wave Ruairí off from the window when the tumble dryer began to make a strange noise. Rushing back into the kitchen to investigate, Kathleen switched it off and opened the door to find out what was causing the din. Having pulled out the washing, she looked through it and came across the thimble she had been using the night before to mend one of her blouses. Shaking her head, she slammed the door shut and let the machine continue its cycle. But, by the time she returned to her post at the window, the bus was gone.

CHAPTER TWENTY

Oisín was catching forty winks as the bus came to a halt near the store at Ballinderry, the jolt of the brakes grabbing his attention. Only two people got on. Jumping up, he ran to the back, scouring the road through the grime-covered window for Ruairí. He was nowhere to be seen. Cursing silently, he returned to his seat. Jono would postpone the job until next week if they did not arrive. Ruairí would have some explaining to do when he next met up with him! The doors closed, the driver slammed his vehicle into gear and, with a sudden lurch forward, it continued on its way.

****

Maeve was late, yet again. It was the fourth occasion in as many weeks, leaving Kathleen trying to stock the shelves when she wasn't dealing with customers. She was becoming worried for her mother-in-law, who had always prided herself on her punctuality. Kathleen had begun to see a change in Maeve, who was having to take more and more breaks during the day, which was not like her. Dashing into the store to open a new box of soap powder, she heard the chime of the shop doorbell. Annoyed at being interrupted, Kathleen went to attend to the customer.

"Niamh…."

The name froze on her lips and she was unable to say anything further. She had not spoken with her friend since Patrick's funeral. Whilst she placed no blame on the family for what was a freak accident, it brought everything back as if it were yesterday.

"Kathleen, forgive me for being here like this. I just couldn't leave things as they were. I've so wanted to talk to you, but the right moment never seemed to arise. I…. I've rehearsed what to say a hundred times in my head, although there are no words to tell you how sorry I am," said Niamh.

Kathleen almost ran to her friend and embraced her, shedding more tears than on the day Patrick had died. Something inside her had finally given way. The months of despair, trying to manage but barely coping, holding everything together but not, it was all being carried away in this tidal wave of emotion.

Just then Maeve arrived and, hastily pulling on her work coat, she ushered the two women upstairs, barely looking at Niamh as she passed by.

The pair sat at the table, cups clasped tightly in their hands.

"I'm…. sorry, you go first, Niamh," said Kathleen as the women both began to talk at once.

"How are you doing, Kathleen, and how's poor Ruairí? Maeve wasn't too pleased to see me; she's been giving us the cold shoulder since, you know…."

"We're doing okay and I, for one, appreciate you coming to see me. I wouldn't worry about Maeve too much, like the rest of us she'll have to adapt and learn to live with it. How's the family?"

"We're fine, not looking forward to the holidays if I'm honest. It'll be a challenge trying to keep everybody occupied. What about Ruairí? You do know he has stopped talking to his friends at school?"

"Yes, I know. Losing his father has taken its toll on him. He hardly says a word these days and shuts everyone out, myself included. I feel that we're on completely different planets, and I really don't know which way to turn," said Kathleen tearfully, lifting a tissue. "I'm sure you must have heard about the guards and that Halloran boy?"

"I knew he was trouble the day I laid eyes on him, Kathleen. They're a bunch of hoodlums, but the father beating him is no excuse for the way he's turned out."

"I've warned Ruairí to stay away from him and, so far, he's heeding me. How's Brendan?"

"We all rally around him, but there are days when he won't leave the house. He feels as devastated as I do, more so for he was there. If he could turn back the clock…."

Kathleen covered her friend's hand with hers.

"Don't…. don't now, Patrick's gone. Brendan's a good man. The animal just had an off day and my husband paid the price for it. Send him my love, Niamh. I…. I'll call him as soon as I feel up to it."

"That would mean so much to him, Kathleen. Sure, look at the time it is, I've been gabbling away here, keeping you from your work," said Niamh as she got up to go.

The two women looked at one another, before embracing again. Kathleen was on the brink of telling her friend about the baby but something prevented her from doing so. As they walked downstairs and into the shop, Maeve busied herself, straightening the stock, not wanting to exchange pleasantries with the woman.

"We'll do this again, Niamh, when I'm feeling stronger," said Kathleen, giving her friend a final hug.

"Sure, call me when you're ready, Kathleen. Look after yourselves and give my love to Ruairí; we all miss him so much. Goodbye, Maeve."

Maeve replied with a stony glare before turning her back on Niamh.

With that, Niamh walked out to her car. Kathleen had already decided not to mention that she had called, for fear it would set Ruairí off into one of his moods.

"Who does she think she is, fetching herself over here uninvited?" asked Maeve, venom dripping from every word.

"Don't Maeve, for once let it go," said Kathleen, arranging boxes of chewing gum on the counter, in no form for her mother-in-law's barbed tongue.

"All I'm saying is she could at least…."

"Are you to go on blaming everyone forever? Sure, you've known that woman since she was a just a babe-in-arms. Those people have been in your life longer than I was married to your son. For the love of God, Maeve, it's time for a little forgiveness!" said Kathleen, in a raised voice.

"I'll make us some tea," Maeve whispered back.

****

Ruairí had left his bike in a field near home the night before so his mother wouldn't hear him getting it out of the barn the following morning. He had watched from behind the trunk of a large tree as the bus drew up, determined not to go back to school before the summer holidays. Oisín was slouched in the seat as usual but soon rose to his feet when the last of the passengers got on. Ruairí could see his scowling face appearing at the back of the bus as he scanned the road for him.

Waiting until his grandmother had arrived at the shop, he set off to the end of the field and out the gate, heading towards Gurthalougha Forest. It was strange cycling down the deserted road at this time of the morning when he should have been in class. Master Rankin would be in full flight, rhyming off an endless list of figures, and working out there and then sums. Whoever got them wrong would be brought up to the front to correct their mistakes on the board. It got a little chilly, so he stopped and, opening his bag, took out the anorak he had brought in case it rained.

On his way to the forest it began to drizzle. Slowing, Ruairí made a left turn and headed for his nana's cottage. It would be locked, but he could shelter in her garden shed. As the shower passed, indecision set in. Should he carry on to the forest? The vision of the black and white barge was luring him in, like a moth to a flame. He cycled on, heading for the quay.

Briege was tending to her vegetables and herbs just over the hedge from *The Johan*, where she could keep an eye on who was coming and going. She had also designed the plot so that she could observe it when on board. She spied Ruairí wheeling his bike into a forested area bordering the quay. He leaned it against a tree and hesitated, unsure of what to do next. Brushing back a wisp of hair, she continued to weed until, without warning, the skies opened with another, much heavier shower. She sprinted up the ramp, stopping midway.

"Master Delaney, you can come onboard or get very wet trying to hide. I will leave the door unlocked," said Briege, before going below deck.

A few minutes later, Ruairí, with rain running off his ears, sheepishly walked into the cabin, where he found Briege blow-drying her hair.

"Hang that wet coat on the peg by the window and I will make us some tea. Would you like a cup?" she asked, tossing him a fluffy towel.

He nodded shyly as he peeled off his raincoat.

While Briege busied herself in the galley, Ruairí made use of the luxuriously soft, scented towel. Then, for some unknown reason, he began to inspect the barge more closely. There were several photographs, some of a more youthful Briege posing with a man in fine clothes, which appeared to have been taken on their wedding day. Another likeness of the man was set in an old brown frame with a thin black ribbon attached, just like the one of Granda Delaney in his nana's cottage.

Ruairí came up to the Bechstein; it was as black as the night, without a trace of dust on it. He lifted the lid and ran his fingers over the keys. Pressing a little too hard, he struck a note and, startled, dropped the lid, the reverberations sounding within the instrument. Mortified, Ruairí sat down nervously on the sofa.

"Do you play, Ruairí?" Briege asked, setting down a tray with tea and scones fresh from the oven.

He shook his head.

"Come," she said, patting the seat. "You are a growing boy, you must eat."

They ate in silence, with Ruairí finishing off two jam laden scones and a large mug of tea.

Briege cleared the table, setting the plates in the sink. Then, walking over to the piano, she lifted the lid. Opening the stool, she picked through some music books before settling on Gluck's melody, *Dance of the Blessed Spirits*. Flattening out the book so that it remained open, Briege's fingers glided over the keys like a feather gently falling from the sky. As she played, Ruairí was transfixed by the melody, its tempo sedate but rising enough to make him want to call out to his father.

CHAPTER TWENTY-ONE

The shop doorbell rang as Maeve came in from the barn.

"Don't you be taking all day to do a ten-minute job, Kevin McGrath! See that those mates of yours don't keep you back!" shouted Peggy to her husband before he drove off.

"I'm going up for a rest, Maeve," said Kathleen, in no mood for the women's tittle-tattle.

Maeve did not reply, still stinging from the unforeseen arrival of Niamh earlier.

"Hello, Maeve, and how are you today? Your woman has a face like a long tail shovel, what have you done to her now?" queried Peggy.

"Don't get me started! Sure didn't Niamh O'Riordan walk in here just this morning, bold as brass, with not even a phone call beforehand to see if we'd any objections!"

"That would be the type of her. And what had she to say for herself? Was that husband of hers there too?"

"No, herself landed in on her own. He hasn't the nerve to set foot here. Kathleen took her upstairs and I don't know what was said but I got an earful for my two pence when she left. This was my home once, yet now I feel like a complete stranger. Brendan O'Riordan walks about as if nothing has happened but he can't even look me in the eye at Mass, the chancer!"

"Now, don't go tormenting yourself, Maeve. Remember, we were walking the roads of Cornalack before he was even born. What you need is a wee night out. Let's get some of the girls and go to the Glass Boat Inn. A few gins will loosen you up. What do you say?"

"No, I couldn't enjoy it, Peggy and, more to the point, I wouldn't want to go and run into the O'Riordans!"

The bell tinkled again and Father Moloney walked in, dressed in blue jeans, black shirt and clerical collar. Maeve's face lit up. She was always pleased to see the priest. As her husband used to say, Father Moloney could bring light to a darkened room.

"What are you two old hens clucking about? Some poor soul's ears must be burning!" he laughed, closing the door behind him.

The women became flustered, their faces reddening as they welcomed the man.

"What brings you to these parts, Father?" quizzed Peggy. "We don't often see you around here."

"I'm making sure you're not up to any mischief, Peggy McGrath," he teased. "It's such a glorious day that I decided to take to the bike. Sure, isn't our best hope off to France for the biggest race of his life? Young Stephen Roche, ah God bless him, is taking on the world!"

"We're all behind him, to be sure, Father. Nothing would be greater than if he brought the trophy back home," replied Maeve, her mood much improved.

In no time at all, a car horn sounded. Not wanting to fall into his wife's bad books, Kevin McGrath had returned promptly.

"Here, Maeve, take for a loaf and a half pound of butter. That man is the bane of my life! Don't go exerting yourself, Father, I'll see you all soon!" she cried as she made her way out.

"It's good to see you, Father, and you're right, it is a grand day. Come outside and rest yourself for a while. We're not run off our feet, as you can see!"

"How's Kathleen? Is she keeping well?" asked the priest, holding the door open for Maeve.

"She's fine, a bit moody, but that's only to be expected. She's…."

Despite their long friendship, Maeve stopped short of telling the man that her daughter-in-law was with child as they sat down on an old wooden bench.

"How are you both coping? I haven't had the chance to speak with Kathleen in a while. Is she here?"

"She's upstairs, having a nap. I'd leave it for now, Father."

"And what about you, Maeve? If you don't mind me saying, you're looking a little off colour yourself. You're entitled to take time out, just like anyone else, you do know that, don't you?" said the old man, placing his hand on hers.

"I know, Father. After all, this is the second time the Lord has called upon me to give up a loved one. I will manage, I always have. You don't need to be worrying about me," answered Maeve.

They sat in silence, lost in their own thoughts, watching as a group of sparrows gave themselves a dust bath by the side of the road. A wood pigeon called out from a beech tree nearby, its shimmering green canopy hiding the nest.

"I'll have to be on my way, Maeve, before these old legs of mine seize up altogether," said Father Moloney, slowly raising himself from the bench. "Age is a terrible thing; too many summers have passed us by, I fear."

"That's so true, Father, and we must take each day as it comes," she replied as the priest helped her to her feet.

The old man tucked his jeans into his socks, got on the bike and waved goodbye as, unbeknown to them, Kathleen looked on from an open window.

****

Briege played the piano as if Ruairí was not there, the pages now redundant as the boat reverberated with tunes that had once come from the record player in the Delaney home on a Sunday afternoon. Then there was silence. Briege turned to Ruairí, her blue eyes holding him in a trance-like state.

"Please, tell me, Ruairí, why are you not in school?"

Ruairí made to get up and leave but the woman was on her feet first and at the door.

"Come, you can talk to me, there is something that bothers you? You did not arrive here today by chance. Not being in school causes much trouble, does it not?" pressed the woman as she had Ruairí sit down again, joining him on the sofa.

In that instant, he fell apart, Briege cradling him in her arms as each sob coursed through his body. She could identify with what the boy was going through. At the time of her own loss, she had had no one to hold her, comfort her, or listen to her. Tears began to slowly trickle down Briege's face.

"Let it all out, child, you have waited for this moment," she soothed, drying both Ruairí's eyes and her own with a handkerchief. After a while, he became calmer and Briege bathed his forehead with a damp cloth.

"Better now?"

He nodded, straightening himself in the seat and drank the glass of juice she had brought him.

"I didn't go to school," he cried out, "because someone wants me to help him rob a baker's van in Birr!"

Briege was unsure if she had heard correctly.

"Who wants to rob who? I don't follow you?"

"Oisín Halloran. He got me in trouble with the guards a few weeks ago, and Mam has told me not to hang out with him. I'm not, but he is trying to make me go to Birr to meet up with his friend and rob the baker. I don't want to do it, so I didn't get on the bus this morning because Oisín would have been there, waiting for me" explained Ruairí, his voice beginning to break.

"You are telling me the truth, no tall tales in between?"

"It's the truth, I swear! You're just like my mam, she doesn't believe a word I say either! He hits me too, if I don't give him my lunch money!"

"I do believe you. And this Halloran boy has actually struck you?"

Ruairí lifted his shirt, revealing the fading bruises on his stomach. Briege's face became pensive. She had seen similar marks when she had been a teacher in Holland.

"When was this robbery to take place, Ruairí?"

"Today. Oisín and I were to meet his friend Jono in Birr; I don't know any more details."

"But they have tried this once before, you say?"

"Yes, but someone called the Gardaí. Please help me, Mrs Geels, I don't want to get into any more trouble!"

"You are not to worry, Ruairí, I will see that this is stopped."

"Where are we going?" asked Ruairí, watching the woman put on her coat.

"We must speak with your mother. I believe what you say to be truthful and I will help you to tell her. Come, and don't forget your raincoat."

With this, they both set out on their bikes to Ballinderry. Every so often, birds would swoop out in front of them to feed on insects. For her age, the woman could set a fair pace, thought Ruairí, as he kept changing gears to keep up.

"I don't travel too fast for you?" asked Briege.

“I’m fine,” replied Ruairí, a little out of breath. “You seem to like bikes, are there many in Holland?”

“Almost everyone in Holland has a bicycle. It is a popular way to travel, but there we don’t have your hills and mountains to contend with!” she giggled.

“Do they have races? Stephen Ro….”

It was so long since he had uttered that name and then it had been to his father. He was immediately silenced, not wanting to continue the conversation any further.

“Yes, we have many road races. Mr Roche raced against my husband in local events,” said Briege, in between breaths, as they neared the top of a hillock.

Ruairí wanted to tell the woman that his hero was taking part in the Tour de France this year and that he had shook his hand. But he was unable to unlock that little part of him, that sacred place his father’s passing had closed so tightly that no key could release.

****

Maeve looked up at the antique mahogany clock above the counter. It was coming up to eleven-thirty, over half an hour since Father Moloney had left and Kathleen had still not come down to give her a break. Not that they were doing much in the way of trade today; the sunshine had people out doing more enjoyable things.

“Are you up here, Kathleen?” said Maeve, having climbed the stairs.

As she walked through each room, she found them all empty but, on turning the handle on the bathroom door, Maeve realised that it was locked.

"Are you in there, Kathleen? I thought you might come down. I could do with the company."

She heard the door being unlocked and opened it, finding Kathleen ashen faced and doubled up on the floor.

"You poor dear! What's the matter?" enquired Maeve.

"I think I'm having a miscarriage, Maeve; it hurts so badly!"

Maeve could see that Kathleen was in dire need of help. Goodness knew how long she had been in this state. The worry of being unable to complete a full term was the main reason Kathleen had said nothing about the baby to Ruairí; he had suffered enough loss of late.

"Stay right where you are, I'm calling Dr Walsh," said Maeve, as she ran and dialled the number for the surgery.

After speaking to Kathleen, the doctor sent an ambulance to take her to Birr hospital for observation.

"Will you bring Ruairí to see me later, Maeve? This is the last thing he needs right now, me not being there for him."

"Don't you be worrying about Ruairí, I'll take care of him," replied Maeve. "It's you that needs the looking after."

CHAPTER TWENTY-TWO

Maeve had just locked the shop up and was in the kitchen preparing a snack when she heard a conversation taking place below, followed by footsteps ascending the stairs. She peered anxiously around the door.

"Ruairí Delaney, you scared the wits out of me! What in heaven's name are you doing here, and why aren't you in school?" she questioned angrily, on discovering the source of the noise.

"It's okay, I am with him," said a familiar voice, coming from behind Ruairí.

Shocked, Maeve stared hard at the two of them, searching for clues as to what was going on. Every which way Ruairí turned nowadays brought a new problem. Folding her arms tightly, she wearily sat down at the table, readying herself for this next crisis.

"Ruairí, please go and wait in the front room for me," said Briege, needing to speak with Maeve in private.

"This is our house, if you don't mind, Mrs Geels, and I will tell my grandson what to do!"

"Please, call me Briege. I am not here for confrontation, it was Ruairí who came to me. He needs help. May I speak with his mother?"

Maeve didn't know how much more she could take. This day had left her drained. She had thought that, by the time her grandson came home from school, she would be mentally prepared to break it to him that Kathleen had been taken ill and was in hospital. In a whisper, she explained the situation to Briege, informing her that Ruairí was unaware of his mother's pregnancy.

In turn, Briege described Ruairí's secret visits, and the bruising on his body from the beatings he had endured from Oisín. She went on to tell Maeve what Halloran had been planning next.

"I thought this was over with after the last incident but obviously not. It's best if I speak with Ruairí myself," said Maeve, attempting to reaffirm her authority.

"Ruairí, come here please, and sit yourself down. Now, tell me, did Oisín Halloran hit you?" Maeve asked. "And I want no lies, there have been enough of those already."

"Yes, Nana. I tried to stay away from him but he wouldn't leave me alone…. honest!" said Ruairí, wild-eyed.

Maeve looked at him sceptically.

"It's the truth, Nana! Why don't you believe me? Mrs Geels does!"

"I do believe you, pet. I'll go and ring the guards straight away."

In next to no time, Maeve returned to the room, having made the call to Birr Garda Station.

"You weren't to know, Ruairí, but your mother hasn't been well for a while and Dr Walsh has decided she needs to rest. The staff at the hospital are looking after her and, when she's settled, I'll take you to see her," Maeve explained as best she could to an eleven-year-old she no longer recognised.

Ruairí turned towards Briege for a sign that everything was going to be alright. First, his father had been taken into hospital, never to return, and now his mother. Because of Mrs Geels' support, he had finally gathered enough courage to tell his mam what was really happening in his life, but she had gone and left him.

"Is she coming back? She will come back to us, won't she?" he asked, panic setting in.

Ruairí's lower lip trembled and he ran to Briege who took his hand, squeezing it tightly. Feeling rejected, Maeve could only look on as Briege gently shook her head in attempt to reassure the old woman that everything would be fine.

"I must speak with your grandmother, Ruairí, so would you please go into the front room for a minute or two and close the door on your way out. Oh, and don't look so glum, little lamb," Briege said as doubt seemed to creep over him, "we just have a few matters that need addressing. If you like, I will go with you to see your mother. Deal?"

She smiled brightly.

"Deal!" he replied, leaving them alone to talk.

"May I call you Maeve?" asked Briege.

"Mrs Delaney is fine if you don't mind. I'm much obliged to you for bringing Ruairí home, but you can go now. I'll take it from here."

"Mrs Delaney, may I say one more thing?"

"If you must."

"I'm not here to interfere or cause trouble, I only came out of concern for your grandson."

"That is as may be, but his mother and I are doing our utmost for Ruairí. Admittedly, it has not been easy to talk to him, what with one thing and another, and Ruairí has been a little economical with the truth lately."

"Mrs Delaney, you have my deepest sympathy," Briege replied, "but perhaps Ruairí felt he had no voice at home?"

Maeve had heard enough and decided to turn the conversation to the Dutchwoman's past.

"What was your maiden name, if I may be so bold as to ask?"

"It was de Wit."

"So, you are the daughter of Anders de Wit?"

"You remember my family?"

"Indeed I do. Your mother was a fine person, though what she saw in your father I'll never know! What he did to many of the people in the area was nothing short of criminal; he nearly bankrupted some of the folks round here. So, you see, I don't need any lectures from the likes of you on housekeeping!"

"I was only seven years old then, Mrs Delaney. I may be my father's daughter, but I am not like him. We were told by my mother that papa had been homesick and, without any discussion, our family was uprooted and taken back to Holland. I only heard about all the unpaid bills he had left here, when I was much older."

"Why did you come back after all this time? The shamrock pulling at your heartstrings, was it?" asked Maeve, with more than a hint of sarcasm in her voice.

There was an uncomfortable silence before Briege eventually answered.

"Two years ago, my husband Johan and I were enjoying an evening stroll near our barge, which was moored at a jetty south of Rotterdam. We had been out for a meal; it's always that last meal you remember. Usually we would have hailed a taxi cab but, on this occasion, we decided to walk off our desserts. Some two hundred metres later we encountered a youth - he was high on drugs - who ordered us to hand over our money and jewellery. We didn't argue and began removing what we had on us but something, I don't know what, spooked him. He lunged at me and Johan tried to block him but suffered a fatal stab wound."

"I am so sorry, I didn't know. Please forgive my insensitivity, I had no right prying into your personal life."

"Believe me, I'm grateful that you did. At least it will put the gossips, people like Mr Hewitt, straight. I have heard so many tales as to why I came back to live here. Now you know I am a local, in every sense of the word. If I can help during these challenging times, just say; losing someone close is hard to get over."

Maeve felt so ashamed. Ever since Briege had arrived at Coolbawn, she had done nothing but malign her for her father's wrongdoings over thirty years ago, when the greatest crime this poor woman had committed was to return to her homeland.

"Have you ever worked in a shop, Briege?"

Both women burst out laughing at the thought. A few hours ago, she had been the strange Dutchwoman who lived on the boat alone. Now, here they were preparing bacon, egg and chips for their supper.

****

That night, Ruairí lay with the bedcovers off and the window open, allowing a light breeze to wander in. Met Éireann had got it right, and July's simmering heat was turning the house into a fiery cauldron. Nana and Mrs Geels had been talking for hours, their hysterical laughter dulled only by the floorboards creaking as the spirits of 1916 ambled around on their nocturnal stroll. He climbed out of bed and knelt by the window, making the sign of the cross.

"Dear God, please forgive me for causing Mam so much trouble that she has become poorly. Let the doctors and nurses at the hospital make her better and send her home to us soon. I'm sorry, God, it's just that I get so confused and do things I would never have done if Dad had been here. I didn't mean to make Mam ill and I promise that things will be different from now on."

Ruairí said ten Our Fathers and six Hail Marys, placing his hand on the image of the Sacred Heart before getting back into his bed.

The next day, the Gardaí came and took a statement from a very nervous Ruairí as Briege and Maeve looked on, so proud of him. They were all assured that Oisín would be brought in for questioning immediately, having previously been cautioned for the attempted robbery at the convenience store in Birr.

****

As soon as Kathleen's condition had stabilised, Maeve drove Ruairí up to the hospital. It had been a while since he was last in one. He didn't like the smell, plus his shoes were making a squeaking noise as he walked along the corridors. He thought people were watching his every step. A stern looking matron came out to greet them but quickly smiled at Ruairí.

"How are you, my wee man?" asked Kathleen as she tried to hug him.

There were tubes and wires everywhere, and her arms were bruised as a result of the intravenous medications that were being administered.

"I'm fine, Mam, but where did you get those marks? Did someone thump you as well?"

"No, silly! The doctor has to give me medicine to make me better. It flows through these tubes and, as for the marks, don't you be worrying, they'll fade," replied his mother.

"Have they said when you will be getting out, Kathleen?" asked Maeve, sitting down and resting her handbag on her lap.

"No, but I hope I won't be here be for much longer. If my iron levels keep improving, I should be home in a week or so," Kathleen explained.

Ruairí was sent up the corridor to the shop while the women discussed women's things. There was a wide selection of daily papers, books and other publications for sale, and a front-page article caught his eye. In bold, black writing, the headline stated that Stephen Roche had arrived at his training camp in preparation for the Tour de France. The race was due to start in a week's time.

Sadness overcame Ruairí. The corridor was full of people coming and going but, without his father, there was no one with whom he could share the news.

****

"How are you getting on, Maeve?"

"I'm muddling through somehow, Kathleen, and Ruairí lends a hand as much as possible."

"We can ask around, perhaps get someone in to help out if it all becomes too much for you," said Kathleen, studying her mother-in-law who looked jaded and run-down.

"I was wanting to talk to you about that, now that Ruairí's out of earshot. I've asked Briege Geels to help out in the shop and, before you start, it will be just a few hours a week to see how it goes," said Maeve tentatively.

Kathleen attempted to raise herself up from the hospital bed.

"For goodness sake, Maeve, you're the last person I thought would let a stranger come into our lives right now! You know nothing about her. And Ruairí, did you consider him at all? Why didn't you run it past me first before making such a decision?"

"Please, calm yourself, Kathleen, you're supposed to be resting! I have spoken at length with Ruairí. I could have cried when he told me that he felt more contented with Briege than he did with you or me, given the atmosphere at home. He's a lot happier with her around, surely you can see it in him? I asked him to say nothing about her working in the shop until I had discussed it with you."

Maeve went on to tell Kathleen almost everything that had been happening, purposely leaving out the part about Ruairí being beaten up so as not to distress her further. They spoke for the little time they had alone of what to do about Oisín Halloran and how to keep Ruairí safe. Kathleen resigned herself to the fact that Maeve could not manage both the store and Ruairí's problems on her own.

"Look, Maeve, I'm not exactly jumping for joy about Briege Geels working in the shop so I want you to put an advert on the church noticeboard for a temporary assistant. Will you at least do that for me?"

Maeve nodded meekly, while crossing her fingers behind her back.

"Shush, the wee man's coming!" said Kathleen, putting on a smile for her son.

Ruairí returned to the ward with the gift of a Mars Bar for his mother and gave her a big hug, as the nurses began asking them to leave to allow the doctors to carry out their rounds.

"You will be good, won't you, Ruairí? And don't be bothering Mrs Geels! Your nana can't do without her, so she has agreed to help us out for a while. I know it's going to be a long summer for you, but we'll try and get away before school starts again," Kathleen promised.

"It's okay, Mam, I'm helping around the shop, and keeping everything clean and tidy so you won't catch any more germs. Just get better, please. I'm saying my prayers every night," said Ruairí, kissing his mother's cheek.

****

Kathleen had a lump in her throat as her son left the ward with his grandmother, hand in hand. She felt so guilty keeping the truth from him, her wee boy believing she had picked up a bug in the house. She wanted so much to tell Ruairí that he was to have a brother or a sister but the doctors, while having told Kathleen that she was making great progress, still advised her she was not quite out of danger yet.

CHAPTER TWENTY-THREE

"Ruairí, would you please fetch some more potatoes from the store?" asked Briege, who was busily packing a customer's bag with groceries.

It had been over a week since Briege had come to work in the shop. A quiet word from Doctor Walsh, who had voiced his concern over Maeve's well-being, had finally caused Kathleen to relent. Briege had ordered Maeve to see the doctor after a feeling of light-headedness had persisted and, having checked her over, Doctor Walsh found her blood pressure to be lower than normal. Worried about her mother-in-law's health, Kathleen agreed to let Briege stay on.

Ruairí brought two bags at a time and placed them on the rack along with the other vegetables. Oisín Halloran and school seemed but a distant memory to him. Oisín had once again been put into care and Jono was currently on bail, having been caught in possession of drugs. When Ruairí had last been at the hospital, the doctors were evasive when he asked if his mam would be well enough to return home soon and this bothered him. But it was not all bad. Mrs Geels was a pleasure to be with, and working in the shop took his mind off things. Sometimes, Briege would bring her overnight bag, just to be there when Maeve was feeling poorly.

The bell sounded and John Hewitt walked in, dressed in a white shirt, beige chinos, and navy sports jacket. Unaware of his neighbour's presence, he began to pick out the items on his shopping list. Briege patiently waited, tidying a rack of greetings cards near the counter, unsure of the reception she would receive.

"Good day, Mr Hewitt," she said amiably as the man placed his basket on the counter.

"You, eh!" he replied in a haughty English accent. "I wondered when you would start ingratiating yourself with the locals!"

Briege ignored the comment, as Ruairí looked up from trimming the cabbages, and carried on entering the goods in the till.

"That will be seventeen punts, twenty, please. Do you need help with packing your bag?"

"No, I am quite capable of doing that myself, thank you. Put the change in the St. Vincent de Paul box," he replied, cramming groceries into the bags he had brought and then storming out of the store.

Briege watched as the man stopped to glower at her before getting into his car and driving off. Ruairí exchanged a look with her, silently praying that she wouldn't go straight back to her boat and leave them all for good.

"He's such a silly person, isn't he?" Briege laughed, easing the knot in Ruairí's stomach.

"He chased my friends and me off the quay once, just for asking him about his life and sailing on the high seas!"

"That wasn't very sociable of him."

"Mam says he's full of his own self-importance."

"Your mother is a clever lady to see that. I have met many people like him in my time. If you are not strong and face up to them, they will walk all over you. Mr Hewitt is just one small fish in a big pond and there are more important things in life. Would you like to come to the boat tonight? I have a hammock you could sleep in."

"What's a hammock?"

Briege smiled, touched by an innocence so rare she longed to capture it in one of her many coloured miniature bottles in her cabinet onboard *The Johan*.

"Why are you always so happy, Briege?"

"Because I have my own little fairy, who sprinkles magic dust when I'm feeling down. She's right over there, at the fridge!"

Ruairí turned around, ever so slowly, trying to catch a glimpse of the magical creature.

"That's cheating, mister! She's my fairy so nobody else can see her. Well now, a hammock is a bed for sailors when they're out at sea; it moves with the flow of the waves. I'll bet none of your friends have ever slept in one! Maeve, with your permission, I've invited Ruairí to join me on *The Johan* tonight," Briege said as Maeve came downstairs.

"We would not want to be putting you out, Briege, I can manage."

"Nana, please let me stay on the boat tonight! There's a hammock for me to sleep in, and I'll pack my own bag! Please let me go, please!" badgered Ruairí.

"Are you sure, Briege? You have been so kind already that I wouldn't want to impose on you."

"I would enjoy the company, so you'd really be doing me the favour, Maeve."

Ruairí was already thundering upstairs to pack for this great adventure. Maeve was secretly relieved. This last week or more had been almost too much for her but she had told no one. It had been such a blessing to have Briege there. They had talked so much of the past, with Briege jogging her memory about a swimming gala she had taken part in on the Derg when she was in her teens.

Her thoughts went to Father Moloney, then a young man in his prime, cutting through the choppy waters of Lough Derg. He was a length ahead of all the other men taking part in the main swimming event of the day. Many a girl - Maeve included - had been left distraught when he announced that he was to enter into the priesthood.

Those were the days. Summers without end, spent walking the roads arm in arm with her friends. Immature young men, trying to be clever as they leapt from hedgerows, scaring the daylights out of them, pulling their hair or, worse, throwing frogspawn in a childish attempt to gain attention. Bygone times, vanished along with erstwhile acquaintances who had since departed to God's green pastures.

****

Briege and Ruairí made their way along the quay on their bikes. John Hewitt was hosing down his boat but turned the other way as they approached.

"Good evening," said Briege politely, but with a hint of devilment as they passed by, her greeting met with a stony silence.

"Mr Hewitt's rude not to answer you, Mrs Geels," said Ruairí as he leaned his bike against the hawthorn hedge.

"It's okay, Ruairí, I knew he would not answer but we cannot be discourteous like him, can we?" she replied as she locked both of their cycles to the thick branches.

"No," he agreed, lifting his holdall.

Once onboard, Briege went to the old stove and cleaned it out, in order to heat water so that her guest could take a shower.

"Go out to the garden and fetch me some kindling please, Ruairí," she asked, putting the ash in a plastic carrier bag.

When the firewood had caught alight, she placed a chair by the sink so that Ruairí could help her with the preparations for their supper.

"Do you like stew?"

"It's my favourite. Mam and Dad…."

Ruairí fell silent as he peeled a potato.

"Come, it is good to talk about those who have gone before us. Dry your hands and follow me," she said as she led him over to the cabinet. Lifting the framed photo with the black ribbon on it, she began to explain her own loss. "This was my Johan, who was taken from me. A moment of extreme recklessness at the hands of a stranger, and my life changed forever."

Ruairí didn't know what to say. His cheerful mood began to disappear, back to the darkness that would keep enveloping him.

"We were together for over twenty years. They were the happiest days of my life, Ruairí. That is why you should not shut out the past. Those who have left us are all around. You just have to let go, then you will feel them brush past you, and hear them whisper in your ear. As you sleep at night, they will watch over you."

"What's the black ribbon for?" asked Ruairí, running his fingers over it.

"It is a symbol of remembrance, that we do not forget who that person was and what they still mean to us. I never met your father but, looking at you, he must have been a great man. You should always celebrate who he was. If you don't feel like speaking to us grown-ups, talk to the friendly sparrow; he is such a chatterbox that he will tell everyone he meets what a remarkable man Patrick Delaney was!"

"But why did he have to go, Mrs Geels?"

"I'm sure he did not want to leave you and your mother, and that he was sad he could not say goodbye to you both. Remember, it is also hard for your grandmother, he was her only son, just like you. We all share this thing called grief and we can struggle with it in different ways. But the main thing is not to throw away your memories, they are what help us through these times."

Back at the sink, they continued to prepare the dinner and, while it cooked, they went on deck to catch the last rays of the sun. Briege poured herself a glass of Riesling, sipping it as she relaxed for a while. Ruairí, with blackcurrant juice, followed suit. Hewitt had lifted anchor, embarking on his annual summer voyage of Ireland, the crew of *The Johan* saluting him as he passed them by. He chose to look the other way, ignoring them both.

Ruairí thought over what Mrs Geels had said. He wanted so much to have been able to at least say goodbye to his father. There were so many things he would have liked to tell him and so many things had been left undone. The greying mist clouding his mind began to drift away. Tearing up his prized magazines, and being hurtful to his mother when all she had wanted to do was to hold him and comfort him. Dismissing those memories of the times he had shared with his dad because he couldn't rescue him from the demons... He wondered what Aidan was doing now, probably out and about with everyone else. Donal and Liam were more than likely with him, fishing for trout further up the lough and, needless to say, Donal would end up falling in at some point!

Given the balmy conditions, they voted to dine up on deck, the midges kindly deciding to leave them in peace.

"What did you father do, Ruairí?" asked Briege.

Without looking up, Ruairí explained that he had worked around the shop and had reared pigs.

"Did he not do something else before that?"

"He worked in a prison."

"In a prison?"

Briege set down her knife and fork.

"That must have been a difficult job. Where was it?"

Ruairí shrugged his shoulders.

"I'm not sure, Portlaoise, I think, where Mam comes from. He told me all about the nasty people that had to be kept locked up there. I suppose it wasn't too nice."

"He was a wise man to get away from that type of place, it can be very hard on a person."

"Mam said that Dad was much happier when they came to Ballinderry. I only remember him as a happy person."

"Do you not feel a little better talking about him?"

"A little."

"Come, my young sailor, let's find this hammock before it gets any later."

Below deck, she rummaged through storage lockers until she turned up the old hammock. There were two hooks in the room where it could be hung.

"Now, get yourself up here, Ruairí," said Briege as he arrived, ready for bed.

"It's hard, it keeps swinging around!"

"I did say it would, did I not? Let me help."

With much laughter from the pair, Briege held firmly onto the rope until Ruairí was unceremoniously tipped in. It was such a strange sensation, being suspended in mid-air with nothing but the floor a few feet below him.

"Goodnight, little man," she said, placing a light blanket over him. Stroking his hair, she could see he looked younger than his years.

Briege locked the main door, switched off the lights and climbed into her own bed in the other room. As he began to adjust to the surroundings, he heard the Derg. Its waters softly brushed the sides of the boat, like leaves against the window of his bedroom at home. He thought of his mother in hospital and said a prayer for her and his grandmother before sleep took hold of him.

CHAPTER TWENTY-FOUR

July's furnace-like temperatures rolled on into August as Maeve's old Toyota pootled back to Ballinderry. She had just taken Ruairí to the hospital, where Kathleen was eagerly awaiting his arrival. Struggling at first, he was eventually able to manoeuvre her wheelchair to a bench outdoors, and had fetched ice lollies from the hospital shop for the three of them. He had had such a good time, with his mother laughing at his silly jokes. On seeing Ruairí eyeing her stomach with suspicion, Kathleen told him that the hospital had been feeding her too well and that she would need a diet when she came home.

Walking into the shop, Maeve stopped to prop an old, cast iron counterweight against the door to keep it open, allowing a light breeze to circulate. It was one of the hottest summers she could remember and, forsaking her modesty, she decided to go up and change, dispensing with wearing a petticoat for the time being.

"You're an absolute star, Briege," said Maeve, accepting a glass of cordial, the ice cubes chinking off the glass.

"You're most welcome. Maybe we should do what they do in Spain?" suggested Briege, fanning herself with that week's *Woman's Way*.

"What's that?" asked Maeve, mopping her brow.

“Close the shop for a few hours, and have a siesta until the day cools a little.”

“That would never do. Sure we’d be the talk of the town come Sunday, with the old gossipers having a field day.”

“How is Kathleen? Do they know when she is to be released, Maeve?”

“They’re still monitoring her. It’s the best place she could be right now. If she was here, she would only be overdoing it.”

“Ruairí misses her so much. He’s settled down well on the boat and I love having him, but I cannot replace his mother, nor would I try to. When is Kathleen going to tell him about the baby?”

“The honest truth is we simply don’t know, Briege. I’ve spoken with Kathleen about it and we came to the decision that it would be so unfair to tell him that he is going to have a brother or sister when there is still a chance that she won’t reach full term. It would be the last thing he needs after all he has gone through recently.”

“What about Ruairí’s friends? No one seems to call around for him. Is there no chance they will make up?”

“Ruairí seems to have fallen out with quite a few of them, even Aidan.”

“That’s a shame, but I’m sure the situation can be remedied as I think Ruairí is slowly beginning to open up.”

“Really?”

“He talks a little about things he used to do with his father. It’s a start, something that will help with the grieving process.”

“You’re a miracle-worker, and I can’t thank you enough for everything you’ve done.”

Maeve patted Briege on the arm before taking a sip of her drink.

“This cordial of yours is a life-saver, Briege! You wouldn’t pop a few more ice cubes in it, dear?”

****

Ruairí had left the shop earlier and was in the tiny allotment next to *The Johan*, tending to the vegetables. Briege had instructed him in the preparation of insect repellent using nettle leaves. It was kinder to the animals and birds that fed off the greenfly and other pests, she had said. He doused the plants with the mix and weeded all the beds, before selecting a good-sized lettuce and some beetroot for their dinner.

****

Later, he sank into the old sofa, gazing out on the Derg. Mam had reassured him that she was only suffering from a tummy bug, but the doctors’ medicine was taking ages to make her better. How he wished that his mother would come back home.

Despite his worries, he was enjoying life on the boat. Briege was a wonderful person to be around, and she never raised her voice. At night, she would read from Robert Louis Stevenson’s *Treasure Island*, bringing the characters to life in her own inimitable way. Ruairí would make-believe he was Jim Hawkins, looking up at the single mast and climbing to the top in a raging storm, knife in his mouth. With wind and rain lashing his face, he would set about cutting away the ropes and drop the mainsail, ready for what the Cape of Good Hope could throw at them.

Getting up, he walked over to the piano, running his fingers over the fine veneer surface. Briege had told him that Debussy once said, "*piano music should only be written for the Bechstein*." Having heard her play, he believed it; the classical melodies seemed to flow from Briege's fingers and wrap themselves around him. He was particularly drawn to one of Chopin's Nocturnes, the one in F minor, which sounded just the way he felt every so often. Briege could play modern music too, like *Come on, Eileen*, by a pop group whose name he couldn't remember. That had been one of his dad's favourites. He would have whirled Mam round and round to some of those tunes, after one too many pints of Guinness. For the first time since he had lost his father, he began to laugh out loud, remembering the occasion when his parents, both a little "tiddly" as Nana would say, became dizzy and stumbled while dancing, collapsing in a heap on the sofa and laughing until their ribs hurt. Dad had placed him on his large chest and began tickling him.

"I'm goin' to tickle you to bits!" he roared, the smell of Guinness and chips on his breath.

Briege was right. It was good to remember someone, someone who was always there, who never said "later", who did those little things that other adults didn't find important enough to stop what they were doing for. Ruairí began saying a prayer to God, asking him to forgive him for being so selfish, requesting him to take care of his mam and bring her home soon. He would also try not to cry, only laugh, laugh at all the fun times he had shared with Dad, even mucking out the stinky pigsty! Most of all, he would always remember that week in Cork, balancing on his dad's shoulders as the winners came over the line, and meeting Stephen Roche.

Up until now, he had put the racing behind him, but he had found some old newspapers reporting Roche's wins in the Giro d'Italia and being crowned the winner of the Tour de France. Ruairí would have given anything to have been there. He would even have contemplated becoming an altar boy for Father Moloney if it meant having his father back. Lifting the lid of the piano, he began to gently strike each of the keys, their fine notes resonating, only to be cancelled out by deeper ones. As he experimented, he found that one of the pedals softened the tone and the other made the notes ring out. Confidence rising, Ruairí started to run his fingers along the ebony and ivory, like they did in the showbands, whilst simultaneously pumping the loud pedal.

"Is dinner ready, Valentino?" asked Briege, trying to close the door with some difficulty, the result of having two large bags of shopping in each hand.

Ruairí ran over to help her, taking one of the bags into the kitchen.

"I've started it. The lettuce has been rinsed and the beetroot is nearly cooked. Who's Valentino?"

"Valentino Liberace. He was a famous American pianist, a flamboyant individual if ever there was one, but also a great talent. Perhaps you may have similar talents, Ruairí. Would you like to learn how to play?"

"I'm no good, I can't even play the tin whistle in school."

"Never say you are no good, Ruairí Delaney. There is good in everyone, it just needs to be nurtured. After dinner, we will explore what you can and can't do. There is always a musical note within us; it might not form a melody, but it is there nonetheless," she explained, laying fillets of cod in the sizzling pan, the oil spitting as she did so.

****

The following Sunday, Ruairí was relegated to the back seat of Maeve's car. Briege Geels sat up front. Since her arrival at Coolbawn Quay, she had never set foot in the Church of the Immaculate Conception, as far as he knew. The first inkling he had of it was when Briege had cycled with him to Nana's cottage. Now they were on their way to Mass. During the journey, the women talked non-stop about what was going on in and around the area, and who had bought a new car or was living over the broom.

Father Moloney was there as usual. Ruairí noticed that his hair had become a little greyer, although he wasn't about to divulge this snippet of information to his nana for fear of being told off. A handsome, middle-aged priest, originally from Belfast, was staying at the parochial house. Ruairí thought he talked too much, yet Maeve was enthralled with his tales of life in Zambia and all the charitable works being carried out by the Irish missionaries there.

After Mass, Maeve took hold of Ruairí's hand and led him around the church as she caught up with her old friends. It was the same old gossip that he had heard a hundred times before, but with a new slant to it. He was unable to escape their billing and cooing, but the plus side was when they deposited a punt or two in the handkerchief pocket of his Sunday jacket. Out of the corner of his eye, he had spotted Briege chatting with Aidan's mother, which he found strange. He was still puzzled as to why she had now decided to attend church. He had assumed she was a Protestant…. weren't all Dutch people?

****

It was a humid night. Briege and Ruairí were staying at the shop as there was an early delivery due from the wholesalers the next morning. Below, all was in darkness, the only sounds coming from the floorboards settling down and a tawny owl calling from afar. Briege was the first to hear the noise, a creaking motion, barely audible. There it was again, only louder, followed by the splintering of wood. Turning on the bedside lamp, she saw Ruairí standing at the door.

"There's somebody downstairs, Briege," he said anxiously, confirming her fears.

Getting out of bed, she threw on her dressing gown and crept to the landing.

“Go and hide, child,” she ordered, “and don’t come out until I tell you to.”

Ruairí quickly went to the wardrobe. Pulling back the panel, he got into the alcove that the 1916 rebels had used as a hiding place. He was really frightened now. No one had ever broken in before, and he only had Briege there to protect him. He craned his neck in the darkness, trying to hear what was going on below.

****

Briege turned on the shop lights at the foot of the stairs, finding a masked robber emptying the till of its contents. Another individual, wearing a balaclava, came racing past her, arms laden with cigarettes. As Briege made a grab for him, they both fell to the ground. She held the intruder’s leg firmly as he began striking her in the face with his other foot while calling out to his accomplice for help.

Ruairí, on his knees in the hideout, held his hands over his ears in a vain attempt to silence the clamour below but, on hearing Briege cry out, he could bear it no longer. He heard his father’s voice, telling him to stand up for himself for once, and he flew down the stairs, arms waving wildly, yelling at the pair to leave Briege alone.

“And what are you going to do about it?” taunted Oisín Halloran, his face hidden behind the mask.

His eyes blazing with a hitherto unexpressed fury, Ruairí punched Oisín square in the face before ripping off his mask. Halloran struck back, knocking Ruairí to the floor, before both he and his accomplice made their escape.

The room fell silent for what seemed like an eternity, while both Briege and Ruairí lay winded, trying to make sense of it all.

"Are you injured, Ruairí?" asked Briege as she picked both Ruairi and herself off the floor.

"I'm fine, but they've hurt you, Mrs Geels!"

Ruairí was aghast when he saw what the robbers had done to Briege. Blood was dripping from a cut on her lip and bruises were forming on her right cheek.

"It's just a scratch. Do you know those young men? One of them undoubtedly seemed to recognise you."

"It was Oisín Halloran. The other one might have been Jono, but I can't say for certain."

"Come on and stay close to me, Ruairí, I need to call the guards in case they decide to return."

****

The next morning, gardaí came to the shop to search for any evidence that may have been left by the thieves. Doctor Walsh had been called in to examine Briege but, fortunately, she had just suffered bruising following the scuffle with her attacker. Maeve arrived, overwhelmed by the state of the place, and made Briege rest upstairs while she put on a large pot of tea for everyone. The shop was in complete disarray. Most of the cigarettes had been taken and there was a half-eaten packet of ham lying on the floor amongst trampled crisps.

The Gardaí, having spoken with Ruairí, now had enough information to confirm who had broken into the shop and were out searching for the two youths. Later, Ruairí watched as a carpenter unscrewed the hinges of the shop door, detaching it from its frame and exchanging it for the new one in his van. He was glad that his mother hadn't been there during the robbery. She was poorly enough as it was; he didn't want her to be hurt the way Jono had hurt Briege.

****

"Lower the seat until your feet are resting on the floor…. all is fine, you are comfortable, yes?" Briege asked as she prepared Ruairí for his first piano lesson.

Ruairí nodded eagerly.

"Good, it is important to feel relaxed before you even begin to play. Always sit facing the middle of the keyboard and curve your fingers just so."

Briege showed Ruairí how to position his hands correctly at the keyboard.

"How do I know where the middle is?"

"Ah, you're one step ahead of me, Ruairí, I was just getting to that. This key in the centre of the piano is called Middle C. You can find it by looking for the two black notes in the middle. C is the white key to the left of these notes. Do you think you can find all the Cs, using your right thumb for high ones and left thumb for low ones?"

"I think so," said Ruairí, concentrating hard. He began tentatively but then, with growing confidence, found all the notes with ease.

“That’s great! I knew you could do it! The next note is D for dog; use your second finger of each hand to play it. It comes after C and is in between the two black notes, which look just like a dog’s black ears, don’t you agree?”

Ruairí, smiling, nodded once again.

“So, can you find all the Ds for me, please?”

Ruairí whizzed up and down the keyboard at some speed.

“E is the last note we are going to learn today; it is on the other side of the two black keys and you use your third finger of each hand to play it.”

This time, Ruairí didn’t wait to be asked and, straight away, began looking for the notes.

“My, you’re a natural, Ruairí!”

Briege opened an old music book.

“Now, let’s try this piece….”

CHAPTER TWENTY-FIVE

Ruairí had been feverishly helping to transform the house for his mother's arrival. During his last visit to the hospital, the doctors had come down specially to his mam's bedside to tell them that she was to be allowed home within a fortnight. As the day was fast approaching, he fussed with the sitting room, ensuring that it was neat and tidy, with everything in the right place, just the way Mam liked it. Then, with his mother's bedroom aired and dusted from top to bottom, he helped Briege to fit a brand-new duvet set on Kathleen's bed. Ruairí had chosen the pattern himself, peonies, his mother's favourite flowers. When the chores were finished, he went into the store to buff up his Raleigh racer bike, wanting it spotless, just like it had been on his birthday. The wolf spiders had come back, perched high in their webs, but Ruairí didn't mind them now. In a little while, Mam would be back where she belonged and that was all that mattered.

Stopping to admire his handiwork, Ruairí suddenly felt a little sad. He had been elated to hear that his mam was being discharged, but he would miss whiling away the hours with Briege. All those sultry evenings spent on deck, watching the trout as they rose to the surface of the water, snapping at flies, or maybe catching a glimpse of a falling star as it plunged from some distant universe and making a secret wish. Best of all though was the feeling of being rocked to sleep in the hammock on those nights when the Derg was in one of its tempestuous moods. Ruairí would never forget his time on *The Johan.*

****

"Take the weight off your feet, Briege, I've made us a wee cuppa," said Maeve as she arrived downstairs with a tray of tea and biscuits.

"I'm ready for this, the day has been non-stop. Everyone must be stocking up for the return to school," said Briege, savouring the sweet tea; Wednesday was normally a slow day in the shop.

"I've just been on with the hospital and they're both doing great, thanks be to God. I'm heading to Birr tomorrow to look in on Kathleen but, all being well, she'll be coming home on Friday. We're on top of the world, Briege!"

"I'm so pleased for all of you, Maeve, it must be such a relief.... Are you taking Ruairí with you?"

"No. Kathleen wants him to stay here. Have you got everything organised for Saturday?"

"I'm sure there must be something I've missed," chuckled Briege, "but at least the forecast is good for the weekend. If Kathleen is strong enough, the day should be a great success."

****

Ruairí ran over to hug his mother as soon as she got out of Maeve's car.

"Easy pet, I'm still a little sore. You have to be careful with me just now," she said, as she led him upstairs to the front room and sat him down. "How are you, my wee man? I've missed you so much. Did you miss me too?"

"Yes, every day. I was getting worried that they would keep you in hospital forever," he replied.

"We Delaneys are built of stronger stuff than that, love! Listen, Ruairí, I've got something to tell you. There's a brother or sister in here who'll be arriving in a couple of months," said his mother as she placed his hand on her stomach.

At first, Ruairí didn't quite grasp what Kathleen had said. He studied her carefully, and noticed that her tummy was really large.

"A baby? You're having a baby?"

"That's right, our little bundle of joy could be here before Christmas. Are you pleased?"

"Can I have a brother? Girls are too complicated!"

"It will be what God has decided. We can't send it back through An Post, can we?"

"No, I suppose not," said Ruairí, looking at the floor, slightly embarrassed.

"I believe you and Mrs Geels have become very good friends. Sleepovers on her boat! You've been spoilt while I was away! Let's go down and say hello to this fabulous lady," said Kathleen, tickling Ruairí as he helped her off the chair.

"Mrs Geels, I can't thank you enough for all the help you have given us. What those hooligans did to you was disgusting.

You risked your life to protect my son and for that I am forever beholden to you," said Kathleen as she arrived in the shop.

When Maeve had first suggested employing Briege to work in the store, Kathleen had been vehemently opposed to the idea. Now, smiling at the woman, Kathleen felt nothing but admiration for her. The courage she had displayed in protecting Ruairí from the two youths on the night of the break-in was a feat of heroism that had totally changed her opinion of Briege. She knew that those were not the actions of someone set to cause her family harm.

"Nonsense, it's what any right-minded person would have done. My injuries were minor and, as long as I have breath in my body, I will always defend Ruairí. Enough of this sad talk! I have enjoyed working here. It gave me something to do, as life on the boat can become a bit monotonous," said Briege, shrugging off the incident.

"Even so, what you did for my child I can never hope to repay. At least the culprits have been caught," said Kathleen, hugging Briege.

"Yes, they are out of circulation now. On a happier note, your son is a very gifted young man. Mr Roche is going to have serious competition in years to come!" Briege explained, winking at Ruairí.

Kathleen beamed with pride.

"I believe you may be right!" she agreed, putting her arm around Ruairí's shoulders.

"If you are feeling well enough, Ruairí and I have laid on a welcome home party onboard *The Johan* for you," said Briege.

"That's Mrs Geels' boat, Mam," whispered Ruairí.

"I heard all about it, pet," she whispered back, grabbing hold of his hand.

"It's not much, just a barbecue, sandwiches, pastries, juice and a bit of music but if you are not up to it….?"

"I would be delighted to come, just try and stop me!"

****

Saturday had, once again, brought with it a cloudless, blue sky. The celebrations were to begin at twelve, and the barbecue was just about ready for the food to be added. The deck was festooned with orange-coloured bunting that Briege had dug out of storage and additional chairs, on loan from Maeve's cottage, were dotted around.

"Come on, Mam, wait until you see inside. It's so big!" said Ruairí, dragging his mother up the gangplank.

"Slow down, son! I'm not as fit as you, young man."

Taking in the compact beauty and homeliness of the barge, Kathleen could see why her son was thriving. She herself felt a sense of serenity all around her.

"It's a beautiful place you have, Briege, you must be so proud of it!" she remarked.

"Thank you, Kathleen, it is a testimony to the skills of my late husband. Come, take the weight off your feet," said Briege, ushering her to a chair. "Ruairí, if you please!"

Kathleen steadied herself into the chair as her son walked over to the Bechstein.

"Today, I will be playing Minuet in G major," he announced, before positioning himself on the piano stool and spreading out his sheet music.

Kathleen was more than a little puzzled. Her son had started to learn how to play the tin whistle at school but had soon given up on it. His only real interests were Gaelic football and cycling.

With much concentration, Ruairí began to play. Briege had told him, time and time again, to forget the audience and to play only for the sheer love of the music. Kathleen could not believe her eyes, her son, playing a piano! As parents, Patrick and she had never once witnessed Ruairí exhibiting any musical talent whatsoever.

"That was incredible, Ruairí!" said Kathleen as she went over to hug her son when he had finished.

"I practised every day, Mam!" he replied.

"Well, it certainly sounded like it! Briege, I'm speechless, you are the kindest, most generous person I have ever met. I hope you'll stay here at Coolbawn. We'd miss you greatly if you ever decided to leave," said Kathleen, dabbing her eyes with a tissue.

"I have come home, Kathleen, and you are all now my family. Ruairí, would you see to the barbecue on deck, please?"

"No problem, I'll just put the book away first."

As he went to tend to the barbecue, Ruairí found Aidan, Liam, and even Donal waiting by the quay with their bikes. *Briege must have invited them too*, he thought.

"Can we come onboard, Ruairí?" asked Aidan, fully anticipating a lukewarm reception.

Ruairí started to become emotional but checked himself by taking a deep breath before replying.

"Yes, as long as Aidan promises not to push anyone overboard!" he laughed.

****

It was Christmas Eve and the farmyard was bedecked in a heavy frost, each footstep echoing off the corrugated iron sheds as Kathleen neared the house, where a bright light was escaping from a gap in the thick velvet curtains. She had debated the subject a thousand times and could no longer put off this meeting. Raising the gleaming copper door knocker, Kathleen paused at the sound of children's laughter; it was something she'd longed to hear again in her own home. She let the knocker fall three times.

"Keep that racket down!" a female voice shouted.

There was the sound of a key being turned, the latch unlocked and the door opened, bathing the yard in a golden glow. Niamh O'Riordan appeared, covered in flour, and wearing a red apron with holly leaves on it. The two women looked at one another before falling into a loving embrace.

"Hello, Niamh, it's only me. I thought now was as good a time as any to see you all. I've a few presents for the children," said Kathleen softly, lifting up a bag with an image of Santa printed on it.

"God, it's so good to see you, Kathleen, but you shouldn't have gone to any trouble; my lot have enough already! You look frozen! Won't you come in out of the cold?" asked Niamh.

The smell of mince pies and cinnamon wafted along the hall. Upstairs, the children were playing happily, but the atmosphere downstairs seemed subdued.

Niamh showed Kathleen into the living room, where a Christmas tree sat in the corner, its lights twinkling on and off. Alone, Brendan stood at the mantelpiece, unshaven, a half-empty brandy glass in his hand, silently staring into a roaring peat fire. He looked up, surprised to see their guest.

"I'll go and put the kettle on," said Niamh, taking the bag and gently closing the door behind her.

Immediately, Kathleen went over and hugged Brendan as he reached for her, blinking back tears.

"Don't Brendan, hush…. hush now…. it's all over, it's in the past. You weren't to blame. I've done the cruellest thing in not coming to see you sooner."

"I'm so sorry, Kathleen, it was all my fault, I knew the animal wasn't right that morning. There's no excuse…."

Kathleen held him ever tighter, whispering to him reassuringly.

"I miss Patrick just as much as you. We've all come through a horrendous episode and nothing can change that, but it's nearly Christmas, a time for forgiveness and new beginnings."

She stood back, stroking the large bump underneath her dress.

"I wish you every happiness with the little one, and I hope and pray that all goes well, I really do," said Brendan, wiping his eyes. "Thanks for coming to see me Kathleen, it can't have been easy for you. You don't know what it means to me. I will never forgive myself for what happened. If there's anything I can do for you, anything, you only have to ask."

"We must try and look to the future now, Brendan. Let's go and see what goodies Niamh has baked!" said Kathleen, leading him out to the kitchen.

****

With festive tunes being played on the radio, and children running in and out, the threesome reminisced about all the good times they had had, their nights out together at the Glass Boat Inn, and Brendan and Patrick's adventures growing up.

Looking at Niamh, her arm affectionately wrapped around Brendan's waist and a big smile on her face, Kathleen knew she had made the right decision in coming here. Patrick would have wanted this, had he been alive today. She rose from her chair and walked over to Brendan, whispering quietly in his ear.

****

It was a cold January morning and Ruairí, opening his bedroom curtains, was filled with glee on seeing the fields covered in a blanket of fresh snow. Putting on his slippers, he went off to tell his mother.

Sitting up in bed, in her pyjamas and dressing gown, Kathleen looked with affection at baby Dolores Maeve Briege Delaney in her arms, busily sucking on her bottle. At eight pounds, four ounces, it had not been a straightforward delivery. The labour had lasted ten hours and, at midday on the twenty-ninth of December nineteen eighty-seven, Dolores took her first breath and began crying, letting those in the theatre of Birr hospital know that she had arrived. Baby Dolores was the mirror image of Kathleen, with her swarthy complexion, ebony hair, and dark brown eyes.

Ruairí crashed through the door, fit to burst with excitement.

"Mam, Mam, it snowed last night. Can I go outside and make a snowman?"

"Shush, you'll scare the baby, Ruairí," whispered Kathleen. "No, there's no time, Dolores is getting baptised today, or had you forgotten? Go make yourself useful, put the kettle on and then get yourself washed and into your best clothes. Your nana and Briege will be here soon. Mother of God, it's after ten and I'm not even dressed yet!"

Having placed Dolores in her cot, Kathleen sprang into action, and began rummaging through her wardrobe for something to wear.

****

"You're looking well, Kathleen," Briege commented as she navigated her second-hand Volkswagen Polo along the snow-covered roads.

"Don't say that, I'm a mess for heaven's sake! I love your outfit though! Where did you find that hat? It suits your hair."

Briege was wearing a dark red woollen cloche hat with a floral trim, which complimented her outfit.

"Ach, it's an old one I had from home. Fashion never goes out of fashion, as we say in Holland, it just waits its turn," she replied with a smile.

"You do look stunning, Kathleen. Just enjoy the day; you deserve to be happy!" said Maeve, patting her daughter-in-law's shoulder before admonishing Ruairí for pulling at a thread on his best jacket.

From her car seat, Dolores, dressed in the Delaney christening gown with a cosy white shawl to keep out the chill, burbled to herself.

"Aren't you the sweetest wee dote in the country? There's no mistaking, you're a Delaney alright," cooed Maeve, stroking the baby's face.

"I hope the snow won't put people off coming to the service," said Kathleen, a little despondent as she gazed out of the passenger window.

"It'll be grand; the journey isn't that hazardous if you drive sensibly," said Briege, putting on the indicator as she slowed down to pass through the church gates in time for Mass.

****

Many of the parishioners, including the O'Riordan family, had braved the cold and were seated on the wooden pews. Father Moloney had been in great spirits, delivering a shorter sermon than usual, which had pleased Ruairí no end. Even Maeve seemed content, although Ruairí suspected she was more eager for the baptismal service to begin than anything else.

Aidan and his family sat next to Ruairí, with Liam and his parents in the pew behind. Donal was across the way with his mother, father and little sister.

"Does anyone fancy building a snowman this afternoon?" whispered Liam, leaning forward between his two friends.

"By the time we get out of the Glass Boat Inn it'll be dark," grumbled Ruairí as the choir began to sing Panis Angelicus.

"I suppose you're right, but according to my Dad it's to give heavy snow; that means a snowball fight at school tomorrow!" said Aidan, rubbing his hands together delightedly.

"Well, I hope it does snow again and the roads are closed; then we'll have no class. Is there loads to eat, Ruairí?" questioned Liam, his elbows balanced on the back of the pew.

"Yeah, there'll be a good feed; Briege was up all night baking. There's sandwiches, butterfly buns, an enormous cake, and red lemonade for us, so we might as well make the most of it! Mam says it'll make up for you all missing out on my birthday party when we went to Cork last year," answered Ruairí.

"Knowing Fleming, he'll take a couple of doggy bags home with him!" chuckled Aidan.

“He wont be on his own, “exclaimed Liam.

They all began laughing, causing Donal to look over at them with a pleasant smile on his face. Briege lightly poked Ruairí in the ribs with her elbow, accompanied by a stern frown. Mrs Donnelly gave Aidan a clip round the ear, making him straighten up and face the altar.

****

“I do hope Dolores behaves herself,” whispered Briege to Niamh as they watched the christening party make their way to the front of the church.

“I’m sure she’ll be fine; it’ll be over before the wee lamb knows it,” said Niamh, placing her hand reassuringly on Breige’s.

“Oh, I don’t know… that young lady’s not one for the water when it comes to her bathtime.”

Holding Dolores in one arm, Father Moloney stood at the baptismal font with a radiant-looking Kathleen, and godparents Maeve and Brendan by his side. As the cool water trickled over the child’s brow, she wriggled and cried out in protest. The newest member of the Delaney family had joined the parish of Terryglass and Kilbarron.

THE END

About the Author

Terry Hickland is an Irish-based writer of crime and general fiction, and a member of the Irish Independent Authors' Collective and the Historical Novel Society, Irish Chapter.

During the 1980s, he moved to Germany, living in Braunschweig, Lower Saxony, for a time, before finally settling in Wolfsburg. Upon returning home, he created a number of successful commercial ventures before accepting a lecturing post at a local college, graduating from the University of Ulster.

Terry's first novel, On Marian Place, is part of a crime thriller trilogy set in 1994 post-unified Germany. The story was inspired by his time spent there working and socialising WW2 veterans.

Other works by Terry Hickland

ON MARIAN PLACE

On assignment at a G8 conference near Berlin, Detective Chief Inspector Detlef Schmitt inadvertently uncovers a number of intriguing documents dating back to the Second World War. Unaware of their true significance he removes them, even though his heavy-handed approach places his career in jeopardy.

After a seemingly unrelated case leads Schmitt to a bank in München, he suspects that there is an inextricable link between the bank and the documents. A high-ranking politician takes a sudden interest in the enquiry and this, coupled with an attempt on Schmitt's life, convinces him that there are dark forces at play who want the past to remain buried.... literally.

As a poet, Terry has also had some of his work published in The Seasons: A Collection of Poetry and Prose on Spring, Summer, Autumn and Winter.

Charland Publishing